PATHOLOGICAL GAMBLING:
CONCEPTUAL, DIAGNOSTIC, AND TREATMENT ISSUES

Martin C. McGurrin, PhD

Department of Psychiatry
University of Pennsylvania
Philadelphia, Pennsylvania

Professional Resource Press
Sarasota, Florida

Published by Professional Resource Press
(An imprint of Professional Resource Exchange, Inc.)
Post Office Box 15560
Sarasota, FL 34277-1560

Copyright © 1992 Professional Resource Exchange, Inc.

All rights reserved

Printed in the United States of America

No part of this book may be reproduced, stored in a retrieval system, or transmitted, in any form or by any means, either electronic, mechanical, photocopying, microfilming, recording, or otherwise, without written permission from the publisher.

The copy editor for this book was Patricia Hammond, the managing editor was Debbie Fink, the production coordinator was Laurie Girsch, and the cover designer was Bill Tabler.

Library of Congress Cataloging-in-Publication Data

McGurrin, Martin C. date.
    Pathological gambling.

    (Practitioner's resource series)
    Includes bibliographical references
      1. Compulsive gambling. I. Title. II. Series.
[DNLM: 1. Impulse Control Disorders--diagnosis.
2. Impulse Control Disorders--therapy.   WM 190 M4785p]
RC569.5.G35M44   1991   616.85'227   91-50928
ISBN 0-943158-69-9 (paperbound ed.)

ACKNOWLEDGEMENTS

As author, I take full responsibility for the content and value of this book, but I would also like to acknowledge and thank several colleagues who have been very generous in sharing their knowledge with me and encouraging me to continue my interest and activity in the understanding and treatment of pathological gambling. My acknowledgements and thanks go to Vicki Abt, Mike Lodise, Vince Rinella, Cheryl Montigue, Edward Racer, Durand Jacobs, Monsignor Joseph Dunne, and special thanks to Sam Knapp who introduced me to the editors of Professional Resource Press (Professional Resource Exchange, Inc.). Finally, I thank Margaret Groh for her editorial advice and for typing the manuscript.

PRACTITIONER'S
RESOURCE SERIES

SERIES EDITOR

Harold H. Smith, Jr., PhD
Smith, Sikorski-Smith, PA
Largo, Florida

CONSULTING EDITORS

William D. Anton, PhD
Director, Counseling and Wellness
University of South Florida
Tampa, Florida

Judith V. Becker, PhD
Professor of Psychiatry and Psychology
University of Arizona
Tucson, Arizona

Philip C. Boswell, PhD
Independent Practice in Clinical Psychology
Coral Gables, Florida

Pathological Gambling

Florence Kaslow, PhD
Director, Florida Couples and Family Institute
West Palm Beach, Florida

Peter A. Keller, PhD
Chair, Department of Psychology
Mansfield University
Mansfield, Pennsylvania

R. John Wakeman, PhD
Head, Department of Clinical Psychology
Ochsner Clinic and Ochsner Foundation Hospital
New Orleans, Louisiana

PREFACE TO THE SERIES

As a publisher of books, cassettes, and continuing education programs, the Professional Resource Press (Professional Resource Exchange, Inc.) strives to provide mental health professionals with highly applied resources that can be used to enhance clinical skills and expand practical knowledge.

All of the titles in the *Practitioner's Resource Series* are designed to provide important new information on topics of vital concern to psychologists, clinical social workers, marriage and family therapists, psychiatrists, and other mental health professionals.

Although the focus and content of each book in this series will be quite different, there will be notable similarities:

1. Each title in the series will address a timely topic of critical clinical importance.
2. The target audience for each title will be practicing mental health professionals. Our authors were chosen for their ability to provide concrete "how-to-do-it" guidance to colleagues who are trying to increase their competence in dealing with complex clinical problems.
3. The information provided in these books will represent "state-of-the-art" information and techniques derived from both clinical experience and empirical research. Each of these guide books will include references and resources for those who wish to pursue more advanced study of the discussed topic.

4. The authors will provide numerous case studies, specific recommendations for practice, and the types of "nitty-gritty" details that clinicians need before they can incorporate new concepts and procedures into their practices.

We feel that one of the unique assets of the Professional Resource Press is that all of its editorial decisions are made by mental health professionals. The publisher, Larry Ritt, is a clinical psychologist and marriage and family therapist who maintains an active independent practice. The senior editor, Peter Keller, is a clinical psychologist who currently serves as chair of a psychology department and is actively involved in clinical training.

The editor of this series, Hal Smith, is a clinical psychologist in independent practice. He holds a diplomate in clinical psychology from the American Board of Professional Psychology, a diplomate in forensic psychology from the American Board of Forensic Psychology, and a diplomate in clinical neuropsychology from the American Board of Professional Neuropsychology. His specialties include clinical and forensic psychology, neuropsychology, stress management, management of chronic pain and psychophysiologic disorders, learning disabilities, interventions for spouse abusers, psychotherapy, psychodiagnostic evaluations, clinical hypnosis, and consultation.

We are also fortunate to have the services of an exceptionally well-qualified panel of consulting editors who assist in the selection and preparation of titles for this series: William D. Anton, Judith V. Becker, Philip C. Boswell, Florence Kaslow, and R. John Wakeman. Our consulting editors are all highly experienced clinicians. In addition, they have all made significant contributions to their professions as scholars, teachers, workshop leaders, researchers, and/or as authors and editors.

Lawrence G. Ritt, Publisher
Harold H. Smith, Jr., Series Editor

ABSTRACT

This guide provides practitioners with a current comprehensive overview of the conceptualization, diagnosis, and treatment of pathological gambling. Although gambling is an ancient and universal human activity, recognition of a psychopathological manifestation of gambling and efforts to reliably diagnose and effectively treat this psychosocial disorder have existed since only about 1970. Consequently, the research and treatment techniques used in dealing with pathological gambling are tentative and incomplete. Much has been borrowed from the field of addictions and substance abuse because of fundamental and recurrent similarities between pathological gambling and addictive disorders. The shared treatment techniques also are justified on the basis of the rather high percentage of multiple or cross-addictions found among pathological gamblers and substance abusers. Nevertheless, there are also many researchers and practitioners who object to adoption of the addictions model in understanding and treating pathological gambling. They have developed some very promising alternative approaches.

The knowledge and treatment of pathological gambling undoubtedly will be modified many times before it stabilizes on a well-tested scientific foundation. In the meantime, pathological gambling exists and is apparently growing in prevalence. The practitioner, therefore, must provide treatment now based on the best knowledge available. This guide is intended to provide the practitioner with that knowledge and related clinical techniques.

PREFACE TO THE BOOK

Archaeologists have unearthed sufficient artifacts and documentation to establish certainly that human beings have wagered on the outcome of chance events for at least the past 6,000 years. Gambling is an ancient and universal human behavior. Some theorists speculate that its origins derive from the more occult aspects of early religious efforts to foretell the future, some suggest it was used cleverly by politicians and monarchs to distract the masses from the discomfort of food shortages or some other uncontrollable social calamity, and others regard gambling as a natural extension of play and recreation.

It is also certainly documented that, whatever the origins and broader social functions of gambling, with it came the problem, for some, of gambling uncontrollably. The inability to control the impulse to gamble and the continuation of wagering independent of the amount won or lost has an ancient record. Sooner or later, most human beings make a wager, but some of these persons do not attempt to stop wagering until their lives are in crisis as a consequence of their uncontrolled wagering. These persons are now referred to as pathological gamblers. For them, gambling is not merely recreation, but also a problem they are unable to resolve.

The most recent professional interest in both normal and pathological gambling in the United States is clearly a function of the astonishingly rapid expansion of legal opportunities to gamble and the diversification of the situations and games of chance upon which one may wager. From the common environment of the corner newspaper shop where state lottery tickets are sold for a few dollars to the bombastic glitter of a Las Vegas or Atlantic City casino where thousands of dollars are bet on a single throw of the dice, normal and pathological gambling behaviors exist simultaneously. It has become the special interest of some behavioral scientists and clinicians to explain and understand the difference.

During the past 20 years, some progress has been made in explaining pathological gambling, but the explanation is still very much incomplete. Debate continues over a range of issues raised by such questions as:

- Is pathological gambling an impulse disorder, an addiction, a personality disorder, or an obsessive-compulsive disorder?
- Should pathological gambling be viewed as a disease, a conditioned response, or an existential disorder?
- Is the risk of becoming a pathological gambler equal for all persons, or are there predisposing genetic or familial factors that place some persons at higher risk?
- Can pathological gamblers be cured and eventually engage in normal gambling activity, or are they always *recovering*?
- Do peer counselors (recovering pathological gamblers) possess special insights into pathological gambling that allow them to be more effective in treating other pathological gamblers?
- Can pathological gamblers really benefit from psychotherapy for their gambling before they reach a crisis stage ("hit bottom")?
- How effective are the different approaches to treating pathological gambling? What is the most reliable recidivism rate?
- What are the prodromal signs of relapse? How can relapse be most effectively prevented?
- Are there true differential incidence and prevalence rates related to age, sex, race, family history of gambling, and so forth, or do reported differences result from measurement errors?
- Are the incidence and prevalence of pathological gambling causally related to the accessibility of gambling opportunities? Is legalization and regulation of gambling

increasing the number of persons who become pathological gamblers?
- Are some forms of gambling more likely than others to cause pathological gambling?
- How does investing in the stock market, futures market, or high-risk real estate development differ from casino or sports gambling?
- Are pathological gamblers motivated by the possibility of winning money or do they seek only a special emotional experience which they call "the action"?

As we develop more scientifically valid and reliable answers to these questions we will understand more about pathological gambling and how to control it most effectively. Just as important, however, we should also have a more complete understanding of the basic human psychological processes and principles underlying both normal and pathological gambling. I have written this brief book with the model of the psychologist as scientist-practitioner very central to my thinking. As we attempt to understand specific issues such as pathological gambling so that we can make effective clinical interventions to help those who are adversely affected by the problem, we should be engaged simultaneously in the fundamental effort to extend and strengthen our general theories of human behavior. Science and practice should be complementary activities.

M. C. M.

Philadelphia, Pennsylvania
October, 1991

TABLE OF CONTENTS

ACKNOWLEDGEMENTS	*iii*
CONSULTING EDITORS	*v*
PREFACE TO THE SERIES	*vii*
ABSTRACT	*ix*
PREFACE TO THE BOOK	*xi*
INTRODUCTION	1
EPIDEMIOLOGY OF PATHOLOGICAL GAMBLING	2
Demographic Profiles	2
Prevalence Rates	4
BRIEF HISTORICAL OVERVIEW OF GAMBLING	5
General History	6
Gamblers Anonymous and the National Council on Compulsive Gambling	8

CONCEPTUALIZATION OF PATHOLOGICAL GAMBLING — 9

Impulse Disorders	10
Common Characteristics	11
Addiction Disorders	14
Biological Factors	16

ILLUSTRATIVE CASE STUDIES — 19

Case Study 1: Married Adult Male	19
Presenting Problem and Symptoms	19
Medical History	20
Family and Social History	20
Gambling and Substance Abuse History	22
Case Study 2: Single Adult Male	25
Presenting Problem and Symptoms	25
Medical History	26
Family and Social History	26
Gambling and Substance Abuse History	28
Case Study 3: Single Adolescent Male	31
Presenting Problem and Symptoms	31
Medical History	31
Family and Social History	32
Gambling and Substance Abuse History	33

DIAGNOSIS — 35

DSM-III-R Criterion	35

TREATMENT OF PATHOLOGICAL GAMBLING — 36

Abstinence Versus Controlled Gambling	36
Controlled Gambling	39
Synoptic Model	41
Inpatient Treatment	47
Outpatient Treatment	50
Other Approaches	52

ROLE OF FAMILY IN CAUSE AND TREATMENT OF PATHOLOGICAL GAMBLING	53
Family of Origin	54
Conjugal Family	55
Effects on Spouse	55
Effects on Children	57
FORENSIC ISSUES	58
PRACTICAL ISSUES OF TREATMENT	62
REFERENCES	65

PATHOLOGICAL GAMBLING: CONCEPTUAL, DIAGNOSTIC, AND TREATMENT ISSUES

INTRODUCTION

The definition, diagnosis, and treatment of pathological gambling have been influenced as much by the social consequences of excessive gambling activity as by any biological or psychological processes that may have a causal relationship to the disorder. The official American Psychiatric Association (APA) definition describes pathological gambling as "a chronic and progressive failure to resist impulses to gamble, and gambling behavior that compromises, disrupts, or damages [the gambler's] personal [life], family, or vocational pursuits" (APA, 1987, p. 324; *DSM-III-R*). In any case, practicing clinicians should be aware of the implications that the definition holds for diagnosis and treatment.

Furthermore, the terms *problem gambler* and *compulsive gambler* are used often as either informal alternatives for pathological gambler or to designate a person whose gambling appears to be developing into pathological gambling, but does not yet meet the *DSM-III-R* diagnostic criterion for the disorder. Although there is no official documented distinction between these three terms, the *DSM-III-R* uses the term *Pathological Gambling* and provides rather specific behavioral indicators and decision rules for making a diagnosis of Pathological Gambling.

EPIDEMIOLOGY OF PATHOLOGICAL GAMBLING

Most of the epidemiological research on problem and pathological gambling was not initiated until the late 1970s and already has been thoroughly criticized for its methodological faults (Dickerson & Hinchy, 1987; Nadler, 1985; Volberg & Steadman, 1989). In spite of several fundamental problems with the validity and reliability of methods and measurement instruments utilized in existing studies, the results will continue to be recognized as the best estimates of prevalence until more adequate studies have been completed. The two major categories in which the existing studies have presented results are demographic profiles of gamblers and prevalence rates.

DEMOGRAPHIC PROFILES

Several studies have published comparisons of demographic distributions of sex, race, age, education, and other attributes among gamblers, pathological gamblers, and nongamblers. The main limitations of these studies are that they (a) involve populations of rather limited geographical areas; (b) are based on small sample size and nonrandom sampling techniques; or (c) are over-representative of persons already in treatment. Results from several representative studies are presented below.

In 1986, Volberg and Steadman conducted a telephone survey to determine the prevalence of pathological gambling in New York State. The principal survey instrument was the South Oaks Gambling Screen (Lesieur & Blume, 1987). This 20-item diagnostic scale covers issues such as hiding evidence of gambling activity, arguments with family members over gambling, and borrowing money to gamble or to pay gambling debts. The items also were translated into Spanish for interviewing Hispanic respondents. Respondents were randomly selected, and the entire sample was stratified to proportionally represent the New York counties on the basis of the 1980 census. One thousand interviews were conducted, 43 of them in Spanish.

Results of the survey indicated that, although only 44% of the total respondents were male, they comprised 64% of the respondents who were evaluated to be problem and probable pathological gamblers. Although only 22% of the sample were younger than 30 years old, 38% of the problem and pathological gamblers were younger than 30 years old. Although only 23% of the sample were nonwhite, 43% of the problem and pathological gamblers were nonwhite. Although 45% of the sample earned $25,000 or less annually, 61% of the problem and pathological gamblers were in this income category. High school or college graduates constituted 82% of the sample, but only 66% of the problem and pathological gamblers had achieved this level of education. Finally, although 7% of the sample were unemployed, 21% of the problem and pathological gamblers were unemployed at the time of the survey. These differences in distributions between the entire sample and the problem and pathological gamblers were evaluated statistically using chi-square. Differences for each of the five variables had an alpha level equal to or greater than .01.

Lieberman (1988) has presented findings from a survey of 401 respondents living in the New York City area. The study employed a nonrandom convenience sample and a questionnaire designed to develop baseline data descriptive of persons who gamble. Lieberman has demonstrated that the study sample is not so dissimilar from the actual New York City population regarding the demographic variables analyzed to have created serious sampling bias. Approximately 68% of the entire sample said they had gambled in some form during the past 6 months. Although 40% of the nongamblers were male, 54% of the gamblers were male. Also, 74% of the problem gamblers were male. Although 52% of the nongamblers were under 30 years old, 38% of the gamblers were in this age group. Approximately 42% of the problem gamblers were under 30 years old. Forty-six percent of the nongamblers were nonwhite, while 61% of the gamblers were nonwhite. Only 39% of the problem gamblers were nonwhite. Lieberman also claims, without providing complete data, that persons with only 4 years of high school or less are more likely to be problem gamblers than those with more education. He does not provide data on income or employment.

In a report of preliminary findings on three of five states included in a 3-year study of gambling activity, Volberg (1989) reports that problem and pathological gamblers are more likely to be adult males, younger than 30 years old, and white. These findings are based on New Jersey, Maryland, and Iowa only. She cautions, however, that in addition to the prevailing profile presented previously, a significant number of problem and pathological gamblers are female, nonwhite, and adolescent. A complete and final report on results from all five states is not expected until early 1992.

PREVALENCE RATES

The most frequently cited prevalence rates of pathological gambling were calculated from the results of a survey conducted by the University of Michigan's Institute for Social Research as a part of a larger research project for the Commission on the Review of the National Policy Toward Gambling (1978). The data were gathered in 1975 through structured interviews with 1,736 respondents selected in a national probability sample. It was concluded that, based upon a prevalence rate of .77% and an adult population, over 18 years old, of 144,129,000, there were 1.1 million actual pathological gamblers and an additional 3.3 million potential pathological gamblers in the United States in 1974 (Kallick et al., 1979). This survey has received thorough and sophisticated methodological criticism, primarily because the prevalence estimates were based on data from an attitudinal scale that made no direct reference to subjects' actual gambling activity (Nadler, 1985; Orford, 1985).

Two studies have reported estimated prevalence rates for the United Kingdom. Moody (1972) estimated prevalence rates of 1% to 2% of the population as "thorough going" gamblers, but he does not provide any detailed information regarding the method for calculating this rate. Cornish (1978) used the results of a 1976 Gallup survey to estimate prevalence rates for persons at risk of excessive gambling. By adopting a criterion of gambling more often than once a week and excluding noncontinuous forms of gambling such as the football pools, he estimated a prevalence level of about 4% of the adult population.

In the United States recently, several telephone surveys of random population samples have been used to achieve prevalence estimates of pathological gamblers. In Volberg and Steadman's (1988) well-designed study discussed earlier, 2.8% of the respondents were classified as problem gamblers and an additional 1.4% as probable pathological gamblers. Culleton (1985) and Culleton and Lang (1985) conducted two telephone surveys using random digit dialing to produce the cluster samples of persons interviewed by telephone. His reported prevalence rate for Ohio was 2.5% of the adult population; for the Delaware Valley Region of Pennsylvania, it was 3.4%.

Finally, several studies have been conducted to estimate the prevalence of gambling among adolescents in the United States (Jacobs, 1989; Jacobs & Kuley, 1987; Lesieur & Klein, 1987; Steinberg, 1988). These studies were conducted in high schools in

New Jersey, Virginia, Connecticut, and California; collectively, they involved 14 high schools and approximately 2,800 adolescents. The results of these studies suggest that 40% to 86% of the adolescents surveyed had gambled for money during the preceding years. Of these adolescents, 85% to 90% were less than 18 years old and, therefore, were gambling illegally. Finally, more than a third of the respondents indicated that their initial act of gambling for money occurred before they were 11 years old, and 70% to 88% reported that they first gambled for money before they were 15 years old. The most common form of gambling for money in the 11- to 15-year-old range is betting on collegiate and professional sports through legal and illegal wagering pools.

Jacobs (1989) has conducted the most complete research attempts to describe the nature and extent of both normal and pathological gambling among young adults and adolescents. Adolescents are a difficult subpopulation to survey because persons under 18 years old generally are not allowed to gamble legally. In his studies, Jacobs has considered two age groups: (a) under 18 and therefore gambling illegally, and (b) between 18 and 21. Jacobs' data indicate a general denial among adults about gambling of youth. In 1988 as many as 7 million youth were gambling in America without adult awareness or sanction, and about 1 million were experiencing problems in controlling their gambling activity. Cards, lotteries, and sports betting were most popular with youth. Between 5% and 13% of high school youth described parents as problem gamblers; these youth were much more behaviorally disruptive. Between 4% and 6% of high school students could be diagnosed as pathological gamblers right now as compared to 1.4% of adults.

BRIEF HISTORICAL OVERVIEW OF GAMBLING

An overview of the general history of gambling and a summary of the most recent factors in the United States leading to the recognition of pathological gambling as a psychological disorder and its inclusion in the *Diagnostic and Statistical Manual of Mental Disorders* (APA, 1980, 1987) will provide an informative context within which psychotherapists can evaluate the current conceptualization of this disorder and the predominant treatment models.

GENERAL HISTORY

Gambling is an ancient and universal human activity. Gambling artifacts and records establish gambling at least as early as Babylonian civilization (3000 B.C.). Organized wagering over the outcome of games or chance events was also practiced among Etruscans and ancient Chinese cultures (Fleming, 1978).

The introduction of dice approximately 300 B.C. allowed gambling to become a more precise and sophisticated form of wagering. In fact, loaded dice have been found among the excavations at Pompeii. The rulers of Lydia in Asia Minor provided dice to the general populace during periods of famine with the hope of distracting their minds from hunger. In 1190, during the Third Crusade, King Richard the Lionhearted became so concerned over the strife among his crusaders who gambled at dice that he issued orders prohibiting ordinary soldiers from any dice play and limited knights and clergymen to losses no greater than 20 shillings. Four centuries later, King Henry VIII became so involved in gambling that he once lost the very valuable Jesus bells that hung from the tower of St. Paul's Cathedral while throwing dice with several of his noblemen (Fleming, 1978).

The words *game*, *gambler*, and *gambling* are rooted in the Old English words *gamen* (game) and *gam(e)nian* (to sport or to play or to game). These words conveyed primarily a sense of amusement, delight, and mirth. Not until the early 16th century did the terms *to game* and *gaming* convey a clear sense of playing at games of chance for stakes or wagers. Attitudinal changes toward gambling and the consequences for those who incur excessive losses is reflected in the fact that 7 of the 13 meanings cited by the *Oxford English Dictionary* (1971) convey losses or other evil consequences of gaming for monetary stakes. The other six meanings have only neutral connotations, but none connotes a positive or salutary view of gambling activity. By the late 18th century, *gambler* and *gambling* were often used as slang words to convey a sense of moral reproach.

Not all organized games involve gambling, but all gambling is related to games (Abt & McGurrin, 1984). This important distinction points to the fact that conventional gambling behavior is a form of human play. The word *play* comes from Old English *plega* (play). According to Huizinga (1955), *plega* and the Old Saxon, Old Frisian, and Old High German counterparts share among their primary meanings the elements of challenge, danger, risk, and chance, all relating to a central common meaning called the *play-sphere* in which there is a contest over some valued moral issue or material object. An underlying semantic relationship exists between *play* and *contest* which extends from "trifling games" to "bloody and moral strife" all "comprised, together with play proper, in the single fundamental idea of a struggle with fate limited by certain rules" (Huizinga, pp. 40-41).

Gambling has been an integral part of American society from colonial times. Early Americans enthusiastically bet on horse races, dog and cock fights, and lotteries even though gambling generally was condemned as a moral vice. This early emphasis on the immoral and sinful nature of gambling was reinforced through formal legal systems as each of the original 13 states adopted English law into American judicial process between 1776 and 1784. This was then interpreted in American courts by American judges who for the most part supported basically Puritan attitudes toward gambling with an overwhelming antigambling rationale (Blakey, 1979).

In spite of this early official prohibitive stance against gambling in the United States, gambling continued to be a popular activity among the general population. In fact, the popular support for gambling and economic problems resulting from inadequate banking and taxation directed the colonies to employ lotteries as a means of public and private finance. Construction of roads, bridges, fortifications, schools, hospitals, and even churches was funded through the legally approved operation of public lotteries. This method of financing public works was continued by the states after 1776 in the form of state-franchised private lottery companies. Their general success in generating public funds is convincing proof that gambling enjoyed a broad base of social approval and interest in spite of its essential illegal status. As the 19th century progressed, horse-race betting in the eastern states and casino gambling at eastern spas and along the western frontier became widely established even while gambling laws were tightened.

The most widespread rejection of legal prohibition of gambling has occurred during the 20th century in the United States. In 1931, Nevada legalized casino gambling along with most other forms of gambling. During the next decade pari-mutual racing was legalized along the eastern seaboard and in several midwestern states. For a generation following World War II, legal commercial gambling was confined to race tracks and Nevada casinos, but, in 1964, New Hampshire began the first modern legal state lottery. This second wave of legalized gambling shows no sign of abating. By 1984, 22 states authorized lotteries; New York and Connecticut authorized government-operated off-track betting (OTB); pari-mutual Jai Alai spread from Florida to Connecticut, Rhode Island, and Nevada; and New Jersey legalized casino gambling in Atlantic City. In 1989, the Iowa State Legislature passed a law that allows the return of river boat gambling on the Mississippi River. Gambling on cruise ships along the Florida coast is becoming a popular pastime. The trend to expand the varieties of legalized gambling continues (Abt, Smith, & Christiansen, 1985).

GAMBLERS ANONYMOUS AND THE NATIONAL COUNCIL ON COMPULSIVE GAMBLING

The historical origin of Gamblers Anonymous (GA) is directly related to activities of Alcoholics Anonymous (AA). GA is still heavily influenced by the AA model of treatment and recovery (Dickerson, 1988).

In 1957, two men who were recovering alcoholics and members of AA were being divorced by their wives in Reno, Nevada, because of the men's excessive and problematic gambling behavior. They decided to utilize the AA model of group meetings, 12-Step Recovery, and total abstinence in an effort to overcome their uncontrolled impulses to gamble. Soon after their decision, they held the first meeting of Gamblers Anonymous in Los Angeles. Local GA chapters formed throughout the United States, and, within a few years, family members affected by the gambling activity of a problem gambler formed the first Gam-Anon group, similar in model and functioning to Al-Anon (Dunne, 1985).

In 1972, GA's Board of Trustees invited their Spiritual Advisor, Monsignor Joseph A. Dunne, to establish the National Council on Compulsive Gambling. Since then, the National Council has produced educational programs and materials to promote the concept of problem gambling as a distinct and treatable psychological disorder. It has aggressively lobbied federal and state governments to provide funding for research, education, and treatment development for pathological gambling. Also in 1972, the Cleveland, Ohio chapters of GA and Gam-Anon visited Robert L. Custer, MD, at the Breckville, Ohio Veterans Administration Hospital to request his assistance in expanding alcohol treatment programs to include treatment for pathological gamblers. Custer agreed to cooperate with GA and began the first formal professional treatment of pathological gambling. Simultaneously, he agreed to become the Medical Director for the National Council on Compulsive Gambling. It was primarily through his activities with the National Council that problem or compulsive gambling was recognized by the American Psychiatric Association as a psychological disorder and was included in their official nosology (Dunne, 1985).

The inclusion of pathological gambling into the *DSM-III* was a long-standing objective of GA related to its more fundamental goal of achieving medical certification and conceptualization of pathological gambling as being essentially a *disease* comparable to forms of substance abuse. The advisability of continuing an approach so influenced by the AA disease model is a central issue of debate in the field today (Abt, McGurrin, & Smith, 1985; Blume, 1988; Brown, 1988).

The apparent benefits to the pathological gambler of public and professional acceptance of pathological gambling as a disease are that (a) pathological gamblers may be more generally excused from moral culpability for their excessive gambling (reduced impulse control) and its adverse consequences (antisocial conduct), and (b) payment for rather expensive inpatient and residential rehabilitation services as well as outpatient psychotherapy are covered by health insurance benefits.

The potential long-run disadvantage of exclusive acceptance of a disease model of pathological gambling is that research on both etiology and treatment will become biased too much by psychobiological and medical considerations and, thereby, neglect or exclude more fully psychological and educational conceptualizations of the issues.

CONCEPTUALIZATION OF PATHOLOGICAL GAMBLING

Pathological gambling is included in the *DSM-III-R* under Disorders of Impulse Control Not Elsewhere Classified. The tentative and incomplete conceptualization of pathological gambling as a distinct psychological disorder is reflected in this assignment to a residual diagnostic class. Although research has thus far found evidence of cognitive (Corney & Cummings, 1985), affective (McCormick et al., 1984), and physiological (Carlton & Goldstein, 1987; Carlton & Manowitz, 1988) dimensions to pathological gambling, a precise and definitive formulation of the personality structure and psychodynamics of the pathological gambler has not yet been developed (Taber, 1988).

IMPULSE DISORDERS

There are three features commonly reported by pathological gamblers regarding their gambling activity that distinguish it from normal recreational gambling. These justify at least the tentative classification as an impulse disorder. The features are (a) a recognized inability to resist an impulse to gamble, (b) an increasing physical and psychological tension prior to engaging in gambling activity, and (c) a pronounced level of pleasure associated with the relief of tension achieved by active involvement in gambling behavior. The antecedent tension and repeated failure to resist the impulse to execute a relatively ritualized and intentional act such as wagering led to the earlier general practice of conceptualizing pathological gambling as an obsessive-compulsive disorder (Bergler, 1957; Kusyszyn, 1978). Increased information about pathological gamblers has revealed, however, that their gambling behavior is typically experienced as ego-syntonic. It does not cause experiences of guilt, regret, or self-reproach until the related consequences of extreme debt, job loss, acute family disruption, or threat of criminal prosecution occur as a result of their excessive and uncontrolled gambling (Rosenthal, 1986).

The motivation to gamble and gambling activity itself are not viewed initially as irrational by the pathological gambler and his or her family. Gambling is a highly prevalent, culturally sanctioned, and, increasingly, legally approved and regulated activity. It is engaged in at least occasionally by at least 60% of the adolescent and adult population of the United States for purposes of rapid financial gain or recreation (Commission on the Review of the National Policy Toward Gambling: Gambling in America, 1978). Most pathological gamblers wager within the very detailed rules of gambling and sports events. Gambling environments such as race tracks, casinos, and off-track betting parlors typically encourage or require controlled emotional expression and stylized conduct. The performance of this stylized conduct in conjunction with the intense pleasure associated with alternations of tension and tension release are referred to by veteran gamblers as "the action" (Abt, Smith, & McGurrin, 1985; Lesieur, 1979). The action provides a very unique and predictable emotional escape from ordinary reality and is generally reported by pathological gamblers, as well as many normal gamblers, to be their primary objective in gambling.

These findings have tended to invalidate the notion that pathological gambling behavior is essentially obsessive-compulsive in nature. Although pathological gambling is still commonly referred to as compulsive gambling, even by mental health professionals and addictions counselors (Dickerson, 1984), in September, 1989, the National Council on Compulsive Gambling changed its corporate name to the National Council on Problem Gambling. This action was a deliberate attempt to separate the conceptualization of problem gambling from that of obsessive-compulsive psychodynamics, at least until more complete research and clinical data suggest otherwise.

COMMON CHARACTERISTICS

Several other psychological characteristics that have significance for conceptualization of the disorder have been found to be more common among pathological gamblers than among normal gamblers and the nongambling general population. First, pathological gamblers often vacillate between periods when they express extreme confidence in their ability to succeed in consistently winning large amounts of money at gambling as well as achieving outstanding success in other areas of life, and periods when they experience acute self-doubt, anxiety, and depression over experienced or potential failure. Similar to persons suffering from Cyclothymic Disorder, pathological gamblers often vacillate between hypomania and depressive states. The pathological gambler's periods of hypomania often involve decreased need for sleep, elevated energy level and physical restlessness, extreme gregariousness, and inflated self-esteem. During depressive periods, the pathological gambler may experience substantial energy loss and chronic fatigue; insomnia or hypersomnia; feelings of inadequacy; decreased attention, concentration, or ability to think clearly; social withdrawal; reduced experience of pleasure; loss of interest in sex; and pessimistic attitudes toward the future or brooding over past events. As with Cyclothymic Disorder, the pathological gambler's periods of affective extremes are usually separated by months of normal mood and energy level.

Second, pathological gamblers tend to view reward and achievement through gradual, sustained effort and delayed gratification as inferior means of financial self-support and accomplishment (Taber et al., 1986). Although most pathological gamblers are moderately to well educated and have stable work histories, at least until their gambling creates a vocational crisis, they often view normal employment as a personal failure to be overcome and replaced by the immediate wealth and high status that they believe will be afforded to them through successful gambling. They may rationalize their recurrent impulses to take extreme financial risk in gambling with the explanation that basically everyone wants to be wealthy; but wealth always escapes pathological gamblers because they cannot stop gambling after the "big win." In spite of the importance pathological gamblers ascribe to the acquisition of easy wealth, they repeatedly lose substantial winnings through continued gambling because they cannot interrupt their pursuit of the action with its psychological rewards.

Third, pathological gamblers typically have difficulty maintaining intimate, emotionally expressive, and supportive relationships with parents, siblings, spouses, children, and close friends. Family members, particularly spouses, report that the pathological gambler goes through recurrent periods of emotional estrangement toward them and their children. The estrangement may include the gambler's avoidance of situations that involve extended interaction with his or her spouse or family. Typically, during these periods, the gambler fails to attend school or community events in which his or her children are involved. There is minimal expression of physical affection toward spouse or children, with behavior such as hugging, kissing, holding, carrying, playful wrestling, or tickling absent. Refusal to talk or avoidance of invited discussion with the spouse when the gambler appears anxious, troubled, or depressed is common. Sexual activity with the spouse is likely minimal even when the spouse actively encourages or requests more frequent sexual activity. Pathological gamblers themselves acknowledge a greatly reduced or totally absent interest in sexual activity when they are involved in their most active phases of gambling. Male pathological gamblers refer facetiously to their preoccupation with gambling as "the other woman in my life." Corresponding attitudes are not typically expressed by female pathological gamblers, but in any case the destructive marital effects caused by pathological gambling are very much like the problems that develop from repeated marital infidelity.

The frequent avoidance of intimacy is an intriguing aspect of pathological gamblers because the proportion of married pathological gamblers, and the number of children they have, are similar to normal gamblers and the general population (McGurrin, Abt, & Smith, 1984). Female spouses typically report that the male pathological gambler was extremely charming and attentive during courtship, only to withdraw progressively from genuine emotional exchange and support after marriage. Even so, the pathological gambler's avoidance or rejection of family is usually passive, without hostile or abusive gestures. Withdrawal is initially vigorously denied by the gambler when confronted by the family or a psychotherapist.

Fourth, many pathological gamblers have rather pronounced personality traits that are characteristic of specific personality disorders, especially Narcissistic Personality Disorder (301.81) and several indicators of Antisocial Personality Disorder (301.70). Efforts to understand these overlaps have been important in the conceptualization of pathological gambling. The pathological gambler's narcissism is manifest in a frequently grandiose sense of self-importance, hypersensitivity to the evaluations of others, fragile self-esteem, and a common lack of empathy for the feelings and experiences of family and close friends (Rosenthal, 1986). Their efforts to maintain self-esteem often result in a need for constant attention and admiration, which generally obstructs normal interpersonal relationships. Rosenthal (1986) claims that the underlying narcissistic personality disorder in pathological gamblers is revealed in their frequent use of the primitive defense mechanisms of splitting, projection, omnipotence, idealization and devaluation, and denial as protections against very basic experiences of powerlessness and lack of self-worth.

Although most pathological gamblers are not physically aggressive, destructive to property, or threatening to other people, there are impressive points of overlap between Antisocial Personality Disorder and Pathological Gambling. The features present in both disorders are disregard for social norms against manipulating people through lying or conning (especially to acquire money); significant failure to plan ahead and responsibly manage financial and interpersonal obligations; difficulty maintaining interpersonal intimacy over time; impulsivity; and an inability to tolerate anxiety, boredom, or depression. The similarity between these two disorders was acknowledged in the *DSM-III* through the diagnostic rule that a diagnosis of Pathological Gambling is not justified if the gambling is due to Antisocial Personality Disorder (APA, 1980, *DSM-III*). However, this condition has been eliminated in the *DSM-III-R* diagnostic criteria, and we are instructed that "In cases in which both disorders are present, both should be diagnosed" (APA, 1987, p. 325).

Fifth, pathological gamblers tend to view the outcome of many life events as being externally controlled. Research using Rotter's (1966) I-E Locus of Control Scale has shown that pathological gamblers are more externally oriented regarding the forces that control their lives than are normal gamblers or the nongambling public (Kusyszyn & Rubenstein, 1985; McGurrin, 1986). They typically express a good-natured sense of fatalism through remarks such as "It wasn't intended to happen" or "His number was up, that's all." The development of a more realistic and internal orientation toward personal control and responsibility is an essential goal in treatment of the pathological gambler.

ADDICTION DISORDERS

Finally, it is important to comment on the common practice of referring to and treating pathological gambling as if it were an addiction. Undoubtedly, the historical origin of GA in the AA movement accounts somewhat for the popularity of the addiction model. There are, however, several symptomatic aspects of pathological gambling that also suggest that it may be addictive in nature. The gradual involvement in gambling with a progressive need to increase amounts wagered in order to achieve full tension release resembles the development of a tolerance for alcohol and other chemical substances. The pathological gambler's increasing preoccupation with acquiring money and arranging opportunities to gamble also resembles an addiction. Many pathological gamblers experience extreme anxiety, depression, and moderate somatic discomfort during initial abstinence from gambling, which somewhat resembles withdrawal reactions common in alcohol and drug addiction.

There is another association between pathological gambling and addictive disorders. It has been found repeatedly that approximately 30% to 50% of persons receiving inpatient treatment for pathological gambling also satisfy diagnostic criteria for alcohol or drug abuse (Ramirez et al., 1984). These findings have inspired continuing research into the phenomenon of the dually addicted or cross-addicted gambler (Ciarrocchi, 1987).

A basic question requiring additional investigation is whether problem gambling and alcohol or other substance abuse are in some respect interchangeable elements utilized to gratify a broader need to achieve episodic release from ordinary reality and to reduce related tension.

Jacobs (1986, 1988, 1989) has developed a general theory of addictions which relates specific addictions to each other and to an underlying propensity to addiction. His general theory of addictions explains and relates alcoholism, compulsive overeating, and pathological gambling through the bridging concept of *altered state of identity*. The theory views the continuous use of the addictive substance or activity as a means by which addicts are able to detach themselves psychologically from their ordinary reality and become so engrossed in fantasy that they assume an altered state of identity:

> An altered state of identity is hypothesized to be the end product of a self-induced dissociative condition. When in this state individuals find it easy to create and act out roles consistent with their idealized self-image. Those who have experienced this (alleged) altered state of identity report believing they somehow become "more so" with regard to positive features of their personality, physical appearance, social graces, sexuality, and/or competent functioning. Concurrently, they feel "less so" about what they had perceived as their negative or deficient features. This improvement in subjectively perceived psychological well-being also is said to be accompanied by reduced awareness of previous physical discomfort. (Jacobs, 1989, p. 47)

The experience of an enhanced sense of wellness, which occurs during the dissociative state, as well as accentuated experiences of those characteristics that addicted persons find most attractive about their personality or self suggest more powerful psychological inducements for continuous use of a substance in addition to biochemical properties of the substance that may be operative. Even more striking, it provides an explanation for the apparent addictive properties of a substance like food or an activity like gambling where biochemical properties seem much more remote as causal factors. Persons with low self-esteem and a poor self-image under ordinary circumstances, for example, may be able to dramatically and rapidly increase self-esteem by a self-induced dissociative state that results from intense episodes of gambling. Although Jacobs does emphasize this point, these dissociative states also seem to occur among religious zealots and some mystics who have reported states of spiritual euphoria and ecstasy.

Jacobs (1989) has systematically tested specific hypotheses derived from his general theory of addictions and has reported impressive confirmatory results. He has summarized his research findings thus far by stating that "persons known to be addicted to different substances or activities will tend to share a *common* set of dissociative experiences that, by virtue of the relative frequency of their combined occurrence will clearly differentiate them from nonaddicts" (Jacobs, 1989, p. 54).

BIOLOGICAL FACTORS

Although the predominant conceptualizations of the etiology and process of pathological gambling has emphasized psychosocial factors, there have been some efforts to assess possible biological determinants that may interact with psychosocial factors to determine ultimate behavioral outcomes. Almost all of the research into possible biological determinants of pathological gambling has been conducted since 1980. This research provides only tentative conclusions because of methodological problems related to small sample size, sampling technique, retrospective data, and absence of appropriate control groups. Nevertheless, this research has begun to isolate some valuable working hypotheses which should be further explored with larger samples and more complete and rigorous study designs. Some of the initial findings are worth being reviewed.

Goldstein et al. (1985) report that pathological gamblers showed deficits in the degree of EEG differentiation produced by the subjects' response to simple verbal versus nonverbal tasks. These results suggest that there may be some element of basic brain functioning that discriminates at least some pathological gamblers from individuals with normal brain functioning. The authors point out that the pathological gamblers who were studied had all been abstinent from gambling for at least 2 years and might not have shown the same patterns prior to their involvement in heavy pathological gambling, nor during the time that they were actually gambling. The only variables that were systematically controlled in this study were diagnosis, length of time as a gambler, and length of time abstinent from gambling.

An interesting follow-up to these original findings was inspired by the investigators' realization that similar deficits have been found among children with Attention Deficit Disorder (ADD; Carlton & Goldstein, 1987). Carlton and Goldstein questioned whether there was a tendency for pathological gamblers to have been ADD children also. If pathological gambling were related to ADD, then the earlier findings of EEG deficits in adult gamblers would suggest that some of the characteristics of ADD were carried forward into adulthood. Positive findings would support a claim that the observed EEG deficits are a general characteristic of the pathological gambler that exists prior to the beginning of a pathological gambling lifestyle and is not limited to a particular environmental setting.

Carlton and Goldstein (1987) use a retrospective questionnaire consisting of ADD-relevant statements about the respondents' childhood behavior (e.g., "When I was a child, I was nervous"). Questionnaires were completed by a sample of abstinent pathological gamblers and by matched controls. The average ratings assigned by gamblers to the ADD items were significantly higher than those of the matched controls, which indicates a greater frequency of ADD-related behavior during the pathological gamblers' childhoods.

The findings suggest that, when considered in conjunction with the EEG deficit data, some pathological gamblers may have at least a residual form of ADD in adulthood; this residual effect may have etiological significance for understanding the causes of pathological gambling. Furthermore, because it has been shown also that some alcoholics have been ADD children and have a residual form of the disorder in adulthood (Wender, Reimherr, & Wood, 1981; Wood, Wender, & Reimherr, 1983), Carlton and Goldstein's results suggest that ADD may be a characteristic trait or reflect a brain function disorder common to both pathological gamblers and alcoholics. The common co-occurrence of pathological gambling and substance abuse may also be related to such an underlying trait. Carlton and Manowitz (1988) suggest that the underlying link among ADD, alcoholism, and pathological gambling may be inadequate impulse control or impulsivity. Specifically, they are referring to a tendency to respond in a situation without forethought and a relative inability to delay gratification until there is a sufficient basis for assuming a minimum risk of an unfavorable outcome. The attention deficit factor of ADD is related to the inadequate impulse control factor of pathological gamblers by the element of inhibitory deficit implicit in both factors.

> The term impulsivity implies a deficit in inhibition, an inability to "hold back." And, so too, does an attention deficit imply a deficit in inhibition, because to "focus"

attention requires an inattention to other, competing stimuli that must be functionally filtered if they are not to disrupt the attentional process itself. Thus, both attention deficit and impulsivity have a common property: Both can be related to deficits in inhibitory processes. (Carlton & Manowitz, 1988, pp. 279-280)

This notion suggests also that alcoholics and pathological gamblers may both have inhibitory deficits that result in a relative inability to self-regulate some areas of their behavior. The implication follows that pathology refers to the inability to self-regulate rather than to the specific behavior (i.e., gambling, abusing alcohol) and could be used in explaining other excessive and problematic behaviors such as drug abuse or overeating.

Presently, the neurochemical agent that seems most likely to be involved in the type of inhibitory deficit discussed previously is serotonin (5-HT). Experimentally reduced 5-HT activity in laboratory animals has been found to correlate with dramatic increase in levels of reactions to environmental stimuli in a wide variety of settings (Harvey & Yunger, 1973; Weissman, 1973). Young et al. (1985) have shown that deficiencies in tryptophan (TRP), an essential amino acid required for production of 5-HT, is related to reduced 5-HT and simultaneous reduction in sustained attentional processes in humans. Furthermore, irregularities in impulse control related to aggression or suicide have been found to be more common among persons with low levels of 5-HT metabolites in their brains (Goodwin & Post, 1983).

Attempts to increase 5-HT activity by increasing dietary intake of TRP among humans have resulted in behavioral hyporeactivity, sedation, and sleep (Young, 1986). Some of the signs of ADD (Nemzer et al., 1986) have also been reduced. Finally, it has been found that actively drinking alcoholics show relatively low levels of TRP (Branchey, Shaw, & Lieber, 1981) and that pharmacologically increased 5-HT activity can significantly increase periods of abstinence among recovering alcoholics (Naranjo, Sellers, & Lawrin, 1986).

Although psychobiological inquiry into pathological gambling is recent and fragmentary, the variety of findings presented previously suggest clearly that research in this area should continue and may yield some important biochemical tests for use in diagnosis as well as types of pharmacological interventions that could be included in the approaches to treating pathological gambling.

ILLUSTRATIVE CASE STUDIES

The following case studies describe actual clients who have been seen in treatment for pathological gambling. These case studies provide illustrations of many of the common attributes and behaviors that are characteristic of the pathological gambler before and during the course of therapy. Although there is no typical pathological gambler, several factors are often more pronounced among pathological gamblers than among the general population. They are useful indicators in diagnosing pathological gambling.

CASE STUDY 1: MARRIED ADULT MALE

William M. was a 45-year-old white male, married, and the father of two children: a 15-year-old son and a 13-year-old daughter. His wife was 40 years old.

Presenting Problem and Symptoms. William was referred for outpatient psychotherapy by a lawyer who represented him in a recent psychiatric commitment hearing before a judge. William had reportedly stated to a companion that someday he might have to set fire to his house for insurance money because he was so deeply in debt. The companion told William's wife and her sister of William's statement. William's sister-in-law convinced his wife to secure a petition to have William committed for involuntary inpatient treatment. William was released at the hearing with the judge's strong recommendation for outpatient psychotherapy.

William appeared at the intake session by himself. He was casually but very well dressed. He had no initial overt manifestations of anxiety. He had a relaxed handshake and made normal eye contact when introducing himself. Although he had been smoking cigarettes in the waiting room, he did not resume smoking until after about 10 minutes into the session. He was well oriented regarding the general purpose of the appointment and showed no initial signs of any significant cognitive or affective disorder. He had a moderate energy level and well-modulated speech.

When asked to explain the reasons for the appointment he stated fairly concisely that he had become involved in a misunderstanding over remarks he had made to a friend about collecting fire insurance on his house. He claimed that the friend was drunk and did not realize that he was just "blowing off some steam." He also claimed that he owed the friend several thousand dollars on a loan and that the friend may have been trying to get back at him. He flatly denied any real intent regarding arson.

When responding to inquiry about his wife's petition for involuntary inpatient care, he became visibly angered and anxious. He claimed that his wife was influenced by her sister who had been a constant meddler in his marriage for years. He felt he was betrayed by his wife and made vague statements about possible separation from his wife.

Medical History. William claimed to have had generally very good health from birth to present. He appeared to be about 20 pounds overweight. He complained of recurring periods of insomnia that began in his mid-20s. He also reported that when he was 30 he had consulted a physician because he was experiencing dizziness and shortness of breath. He said the physician could not find any physical basis for the symptoms and William was advised by the physician to get more rest and relaxation.

Family and Social History. William was the youngest of six children. He had four brothers and one sister. The family was third generation working class with strong involvement in Roman Catholicism and Irish national, social, and cultural groups. He described his father as a hardworking and very private person. His father had very little close relationship with his children, but demanded their respect, obedience, and good behavior. His father had left high school after the 10th grade. William described his mother as a warm, loving person who always emphasized the importance of good manners and education. His mother had completed her bachelor's degree at a state teachers' college, but taught for only 2 years before marriage. The family was financially secure, but enjoyed only marginal material comfort. There was a chronic attitude that they "just hadn't made it." William's mother periodically seemed very depressed over the family's lack of material well-being and social standing. She expected her children to do much better.

Two of William's brothers completed college and have become fairly successful businessmen. A third brother pursued a career in the military. The fourth committed suicide after an unhappy marriage and divorce when the brother was 30 years old and William was 20 years old. The suicide left a significant amount of tension and guilt within the family. William's sister married a very successful lawyer and real estate developer. William completed 2 years of college before discontinuing his education. He had planned to attend law school, but could not stay focused on undergraduate requirements. He claimed that he left college because he had an excellent opportunity to make a fortune in a catering business which he and two friends began. After 3 years he claimed the business was very successful, but his friends double-crossed him and managed to rout him out of the business. He then had a series of jobs in public relations, sales, and marketing projects. He claimed that he enjoyed the work, but felt he was not ever given enough independence and authority because he was not a college graduate. He also felt it was too late, at age 25, to go back to school full-time. He took a few college courses at night, but did not formally enroll in a program leading to a degree. He said that after one semester of evening classes he began to lose interest again in continuing his education. At the conclusion of the second semester, he decided not to return to college even though he had received passing grades for the courses he had just completed.

He married at age 27. His wife, the younger of two children from an upper-middle-class family, attended Catholic boarding schools and completed a bachelor's degree in science education at a private women's college. William and his wife had a normal 2-year courtship before marriage. Since she was teaching when they married, they planned initially for William to complete his bachelor's degree and then attend law school. He stated that they both worked during the first year of marriage and he attended college part-time. During the second year, his wife became pregnant with their first child. He said he became somewhat depressed and stopped attending classes because he could not concentrate enough to handle his course work. On the basis of his previous work experience, partially completed college education, and general aptitude, however, he became a customer representative for a company selling large industrial equipment and was eventually promoted to a regional sales manager. In 1980, at age 35, he was earning $40,000 yearly with opportunity for bonuses based on sales quotas. He was still employed by the same company at the time he entered therapy.

William's wife resumed teaching when their second child entered elementary school. Initially, William was critical of his wife for abandoning her maternal role to return to work; but as their living costs and his gambling debts increased, he became reluctantly accepting of his wife's career activities.

Gambling and Substance Abuse History. William claimed that his first gambling experiences occurred at carnivals and block fairs in his childhood neighborhood when his older brother and friends let William pick board game numbers and place their money for luck. At 14 he began placing small bets on sporting events. This was common among teenagers and young adults in his neighborhood. His early betting money was earned through weekend jobs. He bet on baseball, basketball, and football. A paternal uncle took him to harness racing several times, but he had never been attracted to betting on track. He claimed that his adolescent gambling was for limited amounts ($10-$20), although fairly regular. He said he did it because everybody did it. He and his friends sometimes watched old men play cards in the park for dimes and quarters, but he never gambled on cards. Occasionally he and his friends shot craps, but only for change and dollar bills.

At about 16, he and his friends began drinking beer or wine at weekend parties. Much of the drinking was among male friends and sometimes done to impress girls. He dated only occasionally and engaged in teenage sexual activity with "tramps" who were sometimes shared among his friends. He stated that he "enjoyed sex for the thrills, but nothing serious." Male friendship was most important with a strong sense of loyalty. Several of his friends progressed to increased and then heavy drinking, but he controlled his own drinking because he feared his father's disapproval and his mother's lectures which made him feel guilty and depressed. By his early 20s he drank openly and with much less control. Neighborhood bar drinking and sports betting were common pastimes. During his 2 years in college, he drank and bet as a way of maintaining friendship with neighborhood friends who did not attend college.

His first move to higher sports bets began after he dropped out of college in the year following his brother's suicide. He lived with his parents, but stayed out a lot because his parents seemed very depressed and sometimes critical of his lifestyle. He used salary and "buddy loans" to support his gambling. Winnings were spent on more bets or expensive dates to impress females. He sometimes bragged to his wife about his ability as a sports better while he was dating her, but he never discussed details with her. His drinking leveled out while he was dating her, but he still drank heavily when he partied with male friends.

His progressive escalation of gambling activity began during his wife's pregnancy with their second child. William claimed that he just could not see how they could make it on his salary. He frequently spoke about wanting to "have the best" for his family and wanting things while they could enjoy them. These remarks were consistent with similar comments about being the "best" sales manager, finding the "best" job opportunity, and so forth.

Over the next 10 years his gambling became increasingly frequent. He began casino gambling, but claimed that this was done as a part of business entertaining or socializing with his best sales staff. His major losses continued in sports gambling. His wife became aware of his excessive gambling and debts. It created great tension between them, but his wife did not want the children to become aware of it. During one of several joint sessions with William present, she said she shielded him for the children's benefit. William began fairly heavy drinking again about 2 years before entering therapy. His wife complained that the children were becoming aware of his heavy drinking. —

William's treatment plan included individual outpatient psychotherapy, family therapy sessions, and introducing William to local GA and AA groups to assure at least short-term involvement with these support groups. Because participation in GA and AA meetings can be very helpful in supportively breaking down the clients' denial and rationalizations about their gambling and substance abuse problems, it is advisable for psychotherapists to be in contact with several local groups for referral purposes and to be informed about their general membership composition and counseling orientation.

William's individual therapy sessions initially focused heavily on helping him recognize how greatly he used his responsibility for supporting and caring for his family as a justification for his gambling even though he gambled heavily before marriage and before becoming a parent. He was assisted in distinguishing his own needs, motivations, and behaviors from those shared with his family. It is very common for pathological gamblers to deny their highly self-centered motivation to gamble and to rationalize the impulsive nature of their gambling behavior. William was supportively confronted with the fact that during a recent joint therapy session his wife had assured him several times that the family could live comfortably on his salary if only he would stop gambling. The therapist repeatedly directed William to talk about his own emotions and motives rather than digressing to what William believed family members thought and felt about his behavior.

The therapist also cautioned William repeatedly during early sessions that he was not being realistic in his expectation of overcoming his impulse to gamble in 4 or 5 months. William talked about recovery as if it were another challenging game he would win. Often, the pathological gambler is intellectually *at therapy*, but not emotionally *in therapy*. The therapist suggested to William that his unwarranted optimism about recovery was a way of hiding from himself and others his deep fear of failing to recover. The therapist used this specific issue to instruct William about the more general practice of denying one's painful feelings by pretending to feel an opposite and more pleasant feeling. After about 10 sessions, William began to discuss his fears, depression, anxiety, anger, and self-doubt in a more candid and genuine manner. The resistance to acknowledge unpleasant emotions is very strong in many pathological gamblers. Unless the resistance is overcome, however, it is doubtful that gamblers will realize any extended benefits from psychotherapy because of the continued denial of the various emotional factors involved in their extreme gambling behavior.

Family therapy sessions and sessions with William and his wife without the children were used to help the family members become more verbal and candid about family tensions and to acknowledge William's pathological gambling and alcohol abuse in an environment that provided the support and assured control of the therapist.

During these sessions, for example, William was assured by family members that they very much missed his participation in ordinary family activities such as picnics, birthday parties, school social events, or shopping trips, and that these family experiences with him would be much more valued than material luxuries acquired through winnings from gambling. These sessions in which William's self-worth as a daring and successful gambler was challenged by his family's alternative evaluation and appeal to him to accept their love and respect as an ordinary man were very tense and exhausting for everyone. The open expressions of so much emotion and the appeal for genuine family intimacy may become overwhelming to the gambler and family unless the therapist appropriately intervenes at times to provide temporary relief from the intensity of the situation. The therapist should also assist the gambler and family in selecting specific family activities in which they can gradually develop comfortable and realistic levels of family intimacy and support. The family's expressions of emotion should always be directed back to concrete events that they can realistically plan and carry out as a family.

William remained in therapy for 16 months on a fairly regular once-a-week schedule with joint and family sessions about monthly. He became actively involved in GA and AA also. His gambling and drinking activity were reduced greatly with only a few relapses. Psychotherapy was concluded when both William and the therapist agreed that William had, at least temporarily, exhausted the benefit of continued sessions, although he might choose to return later to deal in greater depth with issues that required further resolution. William has since had sessions with the therapist on two separate occasions: once because he felt an increased urge to resume gambling and once because he had been depressed for about a week and his wife asked him to contact the therapist. Both of these follow-up sessions were mostly supportive in content, but seemed to be useful to William. He has not yet chosen to become involved in more sustained and comprehensive psychotherapy.

CASE STUDY 2: SINGLE ADULT MALE

James was a 33-year-old black male who was referred by his mother who had recently read an article on psychotherapy as treatment for pathological gambling. The therapist's name appeared in the article.

Presenting Problem and Symptoms. James arrived at the initial session with his mother. She indicated, in James's presence, that she had accompanied him because she wanted to be sure he kept the appointment.

At the beginning of the session, James explained that he agreed to try psychotherapy because his mother said she would not continue to help him pay his gambling debts unless he was in treatment. He stated very emphatically that although he had some psychological problems, his gambling was not one of them. In fact, he gambled to relax. He did acknowledge that he became depressed and anxious more than he thought was normal and that he had trouble getting along with many people because he could not trust them. In fact, confidentiality was a major concern regarding therapy. He stated that the therapist's guarantee of confidentiality was easy to say, but did not prove it would be kept. James's rather emphatically expressed skepticism regarding confidentiality was repeated several times during the early sessions of therapy. He stated that he did not trust people just because they were professionals or experts. He claimed that people had to prove to him that they deserved his trust because people double-crossed each other a lot. Although James was more explicit and dramatic in expressing his concerns about interpersonal trust than most pathological gamblers, sharing trust is an important underlying issue for all pathological gamblers. They often rationalize their own manipulation of others on the premise that life is one big con game.

Although James was clearly anxious, very suspicious, and somewhat hostile toward the therapist, he showed no signs of psychotic thought process. His reported depressions seemed to be a dysthymic disorder and not a major affective disorder or depression according to *DSM-III-R* criteria. James's gambling behavior also met six of the nine *DSM-III-R* criteria for pathological gambling. Evidence of Post-Traumatic Stress Disorder possibly related to Vietnam combat experiences is discussed in the "Family and Social History."

Medical History. James claimed to have always had generally good health. He appeared physically robust with well-developed musculature. He stated that he had several episodes of respiratory distress during childhood and early adolescence. He thought it had been diagnosed as asthma for which he took medication for a while. He had no further recurrence of the symptoms from about age 14. He had been wounded moderately twice by shell fragments while serving in Vietnam.

Family and Social History. James was the only child in his immediate family, although he stated he had several first cousins with whom he had regular contact during childhood and adolescence. Both parents worked in a small but very successful retail business. They also owned several properties with apartment rentals. James's childhood was materially very secure and comfortable. His parents related well to each other and were well respected in their community because of their business success. They were also both active in their church and routinely included James in church social and community activities. James was a consistently good student in the public school that he attended. In mid-adolescence, he became involved in urban teenage street culture, but was never involved in any significant delinquent or criminal activity. He graduated from high school, completed a 2-year associate degree in accounting and business administration at a community college, and intended to continue for his bachelor's degree when he was drafted by the Army for service in Vietnam. He served 1 year in Vietnam where he was involved in combat for most of his tour. He expressed strong resentment about having had to be involved in combat. He had lost several close "buddies" in combat and had been present when they were seriously wounded and/or killed. He became most intense emotionally when he discussed the test of loyalty and friendship under fire. He was very resentful toward the government for what he felt was its post-Vietnam neglect of the veterans. He claimed there were definite racial overtones to the war even though in combat he and other black soldiers had developed close and loyal friendships with individual whites. His discussion of his combat experience and the nature of the emotion expressed about combat suggested the possibility that James was also suffering from Post-Traumatic Stress Disorder (309.89). Specifically, James reported many intensely violent encounters with the enemy in Vietnam. Close friends were killed and he was injured several times. He had recurrent memories and dreams about combat as well as flashback episodes. He became angry when discussing his military experiences. He expressed feelings of detachment from others and appeared to have a limited range of affect. Finally, he was highly suspicious of others, was hypervigilant, and had repeated sudden outbursts of anger.

After discharge from the military service, he completed his bachelor's degree in business administration. He was employed as an Assistant Administrator in a federally funded social services program for 2 years and was fairly successful. During this time, he married a woman who had a Master of Social Work (MSW). He had met her through his job. Both were employed and financially comfortable. The first year of marriage went fairly well, but by the second year they began to argue a great deal. He spent progressively more of his spare time with male companions playing basketball and cards, and drinking. At the end of the second year of his marriage, his father died of cancer. Shortly thereafter, he and his wife separated. He returned to live with his mother. Over the next several years he was involved with several different women and his divorce was finalized.

He moved to a higher position as Financial Administrator and Budget Director for a larger agency. At this time, he took his own apartment and invited a girlfriend to live with him. He claimed that he was able to feel closer to her and open up more than with his wife. After 2 years at his new job he was dismissed because an annual audit revealed either serious mismanagement of funds or outright embezzlement. Shortly thereafter, he was arrested for forgery. He claimed the woman he was living with testified against him and was a key witness. He spent 6 months in prison and was then paroled. Several friends helped him get a minor administrative job in a social service agency where he presently works.

Gambling and Substance Abuse History. James claimed that no one in his family ever gambled. He said they were all very straight church people. There was very little use of alcohol and no use of illegal drugs. He recalled how his parents and other adult relatives pointed out how black people ruined themselves by getting involved with alcohol and drugs.

When he was 16 he began drinking wine or beer if it was available at parties or on the street. He also used marijuana when other people supplied it, but he never purchased it himself. Both alcohol and marijuana were used occasionally.

He learned about sports betting from school friends and on the street. He also learned about numbers betting on the street, but he only gambled on sports occasionally. He claims his real introduction to gambling occurred during military training. Cards, craps, and sports gambling were very common and easily financed by a series of rotating loans. In Vietnam, gambling was epidemic. By the time he completed his tour, he had won and lost at least $20,000 backing friends who played cards. He returned to the U.S.A. with about $8,000 in winnings. He continued sports betting while in college and during the first several years of employment. He learned how to use bookmakers and loan sharks as his gambling intensified. He began borrowing from his mother on the pretext that he was trying to start a business. He also began gambling at Atlantic City casinos, although he continued gambling most actively on sports. By the time he entered therapy, he was about $50,000 in debt and was being threatened by loan sharks for nonpayment.

James agreed to attend a 1-hour individual therapy session once weekly. He refused to become involved with GA because he said he did not feel safe talking about personal issues with people he did not know very well. His mother was instructed that she should not pay any new gambling debts incurred by James and that her assistance in paying off existing debts should be limited according to terms of a schedule that James would develop in a psychotherapy session. She was also instructed not to discuss James's gambling activity with him. Instead, she was to remind him kindly that he was to discuss his problems with the therapist. His mother agreed with some reluctance. This requirement was instituted to overcome the common practice in which a family member or close friend is enlisted as an ally by the gambler to provide both psychological and financial support to the gambler in his or her continued gambling. The gambler is often able to create a sense of guilt and inappropriate responsibility in the ally for the gambler's problematic behavior. This phenomenon is discussed more comprehensively in the recent literature on co-dependency (Beattie, 1987).

The first three sessions were involved primarily in supportively confronting James with the problematic consequences of his gambling activity and his actual inability to stop. James continued to deny that he was a pathological gambler and challenged the therapist's basis for making statements about anyone's motivation to gamble. James's resistance seemed to be a test of the therapist's professional self-confidence and patience as much as a denial of his own problem. This type of testing the therapist is common among pathological gamblers and seems to reflect, as already mentioned, their great reluctance to trust others - especially authority figures. They also refuse to acknowledge that anyone but an experienced gambler can really understand anything significant about gamblers and gambling. This attitude reflects the mystification they frequently attribute to their gambling activity.

By the fourth session, James was willing to acknowledge the problem and the fact that his excessive gambling might be symptomatic of less visible personal conflicts. He did not agree, however, that because his gambling activity placed him in debt to loan sharks, who threatened his physical safety, his gambling might be viewed as self-punitive or destructive activity. He was more emotional than usual in rejecting these interpretations. In the fifth session, he admitted that he was still gambling occasionally and that he was finding it very difficult to resist the impulse to gamble even when he did not gamble. He seemed distressed by his lack of control and the apparent weakness it implied. The therapist assured James that these realizations and admissions were a necessary part of recovery.

When James arrived for the sixth session, he stated that he had several drinks with an old friend earlier in the day. He would not consider rescheduling and argued that the effects of the alcohol had already worn off. He did not seem to be drunk, but he did seem intensely determined to continue with the session. He began by remarking again about the importance of trust and loyalty in friendships. He then talked about friendships among soldiers in his unit in Vietnam. The emotional intensity of his discussion increased rather rapidly as he provided details of violent combat encounters with North Vietnamese military patrols. In several encounters close friends were killed, and he was certain that he had killed several enemy soldiers. He had become almost dissociative and then stated abruptly and somewhat embarrassedly that he did not discuss these issues with other people. He would not discuss his feelings about these events any further during the session.

James did not appear for the seventh session. When contacted by telephone, he apologized and said he had forgotten the appointment. He rescheduled immediately, but did not show for the rescheduled session. When contacted again by telephone, he said he had been ill and declined to reschedule at that time. He apologized and stated that he would call soon to reschedule a session. James never returned to therapy and refused further contact. James was a case in which there was apparently very little therapeutic success in treating the client's pathological gambling.

Several factors may have been involved in James's discontinuation of therapy, but certainly one factor was his intense recall and disclosure of Vietnam combat experiences. In spite of the encouragement by AA and GA for disclosure and sharing of deeply personal psychological trauma with other group members, it is important to recognize the risk of aftereffects of such disclosures for persons who are highly insecure about disclosure and ambivalent about trust. These disclosures may be therapeutically cathartic or they may create so much self-criticism, guilt, and related embarrassment for individuals over their disclosure of very emotionally intense events that they discontinue contact. In therapy, if the disclosures occur prematurely, before a sufficient trust and comfort is developed with the therapist, the experience may be countertherapeutic for the client. It remains a difficult clinical judgment for the therapist to decide when the therapeutic relationship is established well enough to encourage the client to disclose these deeply personal events without too much risk of the client's counterreaction of withdrawing from therapy.

CASE STUDY 3: SINGLE ADOLESCENT MALE

Tom R. was a 20-year-old white male who had been referred from a 28-day program where he had been treated for a combination of alcohol detoxification and pathological gambling.

Presenting Problem and Symptoms. Tom appeared at the initial session with his mother because there was no accessible public transportation from his suburban residence to the therapist's office, and he could not drive because his license was still suspended from an earlier drunk-while-driving conviction. He acknowledged that he had been in an inpatient treatment program for both alcohol abuse and pathological gambling, but claimed that the main problem at that time had been alcohol abuse and that he had since recovered from that problem. He was attending GA meetings weekly, but belittled them as "just a bunch of middle-aged guys trying to impress each other with gambling stories." He spoke rapidly in spurts, chewed on toothpicks, or cracked his knuckles. He avoided direct eye contact and often mumbled in response to questions about his history of alcohol abuse and gambling.

It was clear that Tom was initially uncomfortable with the interview and denied any real need to be in therapy. When the therapist suggested that there were other aspects of his life such as education, career goals, and recreational interests that they should be discussing also, he became more relaxed and cooperative. Clinically, he showed no indication of psychotic thought process or major affective disorder, although he was somewhat hyperactive and complained of difficulty concentrating and falling asleep at night.

Medical History. Tom reported generally good health, and this was confirmed by his mother when asked about his health during infancy and childhood. The only significant medical event was Tom's injury in an automobile accident when he was 15 years old. He sustained several broken bones and muscle injuries. He had been briefly hospitalized and underwent continuous physical therapy for about 18 months.

Family and Social History. Tom was the only child of his parents. He had several cousins but had only occasional contact with them because one family lived in Florida and the other family had a history of serious quarrels with Tom's parents. Tom felt that his parents put too many demands on him and each other because there were no other family members living close enough to relate to on a day-to-day basis. His father left high school in the 11th grade and joined the military. After the military, he had a series of positions as a laborer or semi-skilled construction worker. He eventually established his own business as a house painter in which he had about 10 men working for him. He was rather successful financially. Tom's mother was a high school graduate with some college and business school training, but no degree. She had a mid-level technical position in a private corporation. The family was financially very comfortable and very much consumer inclined.

Tom was a consistently good student (B+) while attending a suburban high school in a pre-college curriculum. He was also a very skilled athlete who excelled in basketball and baseball. He was a varsity team player in both sports in high school. He claimed that he was very competitive in athletics and always attempted to be the best player on the team. He had several close male companions. Although he dated occasionally, he had never been very emotionally involved with females, and he expressed sexist attitudes.

After high school graduation, he attended a local community college with the intention of studying business for 2 years to determine if he wanted a complete college education. His parents were very supportive of his educational plans. During his first year at the community college, his grades went from excellent to marginal. During the second semester, he cut classes increasingly because he felt the lectures were a waste of time. He believed he could do well enough by just reading the text. During the first semester of his second year, he decided to drop out of college for a while because he said he was bored and not clear about his goals. By November of that year, he was admitted to the inpatient program for detox and treatment of pathological gambling.

Gambling and Substance Abuse History. Tom began using alcohol and a variety of drugs in 8th grade. His use of these substances was only occasional and was prompted by peer pressure. Because of his involvement in competitive sports, he claimed that he intentionally limited his use of alcohol and drugs to off-season involvement although alcohol was abundantly available within his own home because of his father's alcohol abuse problem.

Tom became involved with gambling in 8th grade also. He was initially encouraged by several older friends and a cousin to place $2 or $3 dollar bets on the outcome of local and national sports events. These older friends had contact through one of their fathers to a bookie. Tom had a very thorough knowledge of collegiate and professional football and basketball teams. He quickly learned techniques for computing betting odds and other computational aspects of extended betting procedures. His older friends were impressed with his quick and accurate computations. They began to allow him to choose bets for them. By the 10th grade he had achieved a reputation among classmates and friends of being a very successful sports gambler. He handled many bets for them and had been introduced to several bookies whom he could contact at any time by telephone.

Most of the betting did not involve actual dollar exchange between Tom and the bookies. Instead, he had a line of credit that he could use by telephone. He collected and paid cash to classmates who were occasional or short-term gamblers, but he collected cash won from his own bets only occasionally, preferring to let his winnings grow through complex wagering arrangements with the bookies and also paying off debts which sometimes reached substantial amounts. According to Tom, by 15 years old, he was winning and losing as much as $3,000 per week on sports betting.

His friends were aware of the amount of money involved in Tom's betting and treated him with a special respect because of his emerging high-roller image. His parents knew that he bet on sports events, but did not know the amount of money Tom was betting until he was finally called by several bookies to pay debts uncovered by winnings. These debts were for several thousand dollars. Tom had to inform his parents about the debts and the level of his betting activity because he needed their assistance in paying his gambling debts. His mother claimed that Tom's request for financial assistance was the first time that they realized how heavily he had become involved in gambling. Although

Tom's mother and father agreed to pay his debts, they told him that he had to stop gambling and, of course, Tom resumed gambling immediately. His credit was now secure with his bookies.

Two years later during his first year in college, Tom was under pressure to pay gambling debts. Again, he appealed to his parents for assistance. They assisted him in paying this debt also, but expressed great anger with him and threatened never to assist him again. They did not, however, seek therapy for him nor notify the police regarding the bookies' illegal contact with their son. They tacitly agreed to keep Tom's gambling a family secret.

The family secret was disclosed, however, when Tom's gambling and alcohol abuse had become so much out of control that during the first semester of his second year in community college he had gambled and been intoxicated almost continuously for 24 days. The family doctor advised Tom's parents to admit him to an inpatient detoxification program at a local hospital that also had a 28-day residential rehabilitation program for substance abusers and pathological gamblers. Tom was referred from this rehabilitation program to outpatient therapy.

Tom remained in outpatient psychotherapy for 18 months. During this time it became clear that he had felt seriously rejected by and was in continuous conflict with his alcoholic father. Father and son angrily accused each other of being the cause of each's substance abuse and behavior problems. Tom's mother tried futilely to mediate between Tom and his father. The phenomenon of a protective parent and an angry critical parent is common in families with an adolescent or young adult pathological gambler. Family therapy was attempted, but the father's resistance to viewing Tom's behavior as being related to more fundamental family tensions greatly limited the effectiveness of this approach.

During individual therapy sessions, a major focus was placed on helping Tom define some career goals and in assisting him in applying for admission to a 4-year college. The basic persistence of Tom's predisposition to return to gambling was reflected in his recurrent argument that college and a salaried job seemed rather foolish when he had already succeeded several times in winning as much as $20,000 in 1 week. Like most pathological gamblers, Tom was consistently minimizing or denying his losses when boasting about his winnings. Individual sessions were also used to help Tom resolve some long-standing emotional conflicts regarding his parents and to support him in strengthening a very weak sense of self-worth and self-esteem.

Eighteen months of therapy provided Tom with increased resistance to his impulse to gamble and related abuse of alcohol. Although Tom had relapsed into gambling on several occasions while in therapy, he had greatly reduced his gambling activity and controlled his drinking. He concluded therapy with the agreement of the therapist because he had been admitted to a small college in another state where he would live with members of his mother's family. He was encouraged to continue therapy at his new location and was advised to avoid social contact with persons who gambled or drank alcohol regularly.

DIAGNOSIS

The *DSM-III* diagnosis of Pathological Gambling was based primarily on the social and vocational consequences of excessive gambling, which usually occur only after at least several years of financial loss resulting from gambling. The *DSM-III-R* introduced a modified diagnostic perspective by including many of the common psychological characteristics of the pathological gambler such as frequent preoccupation with gambling and restlessness or irritability if unable to gamble as relevant diagnostic indicators. Diagnostic status as a pathological gambler, therefore, does not depend quite so heavily upon whether the gambling behavior has resulted in disruption to personal, family, or vocational areas of the gambler's life. As a more complete and factually based psychological profile of the problem gambler is developed additional modifications in diagnostic criteria will occur.

DSM-III-R CRITERION

A positive diagnosis of Pathological Gambling is currently justified by determining that at least four of the following nine indicators apply to the person being evaluated (*DSM-III-R*, p. 325):

(1) frequent preoccupation with gambling or with obtaining money to gamble
(2) frequent gambling of larger amounts of money or over a longer period of time than intended
(3) a need to increase the size or frequency of bets to achieve the desired excitement
(4) restlessness or irritability if unable to gamble

(5) repeated loss of money by gambling and returning another day to win back losses ("chasing")
(6) repeated efforts to reduce or stop gambling
(7) frequent gambling when expected to meet social or occupational obligations
(8) sacrifice of some important social, occupational, or recreational activity in order to gamble
(9) continuation of gambling despite inability to pay mounting debts, or despite other significant social, occupational, or legal problems that the person knows to be exacerbated by gambling

As a supplement to the *DSM-III-R* diagnostic criteria, the following 20 questions (see Table 1, p. 37) are useful for interviewing and evaluating the nature of a client's problem in controlling his or her gambling behavior. These questions were developed originally by GA for distribution as public education and self-assessment materials. All of the questions refer to situations with which problem gamblers will be familiar and recognize as relevant for themselves or other gamblers. The validity of these questions also assists the clinician in establishing credibility with the problem gambler, who is likely to initially view the clinician as naïve and easily misled about the "real stuff" of gambling. Affirmative responses to any combination of four or more of these questions is a reliable indication that the client may be a problem gambler and is no longer normally in control of his or her gambling behavior.

TREATMENT OF PATHOLOGICAL GAMBLING

ABSTINENCE VERSUS CONTROLLED GAMBLING

The prevailing goal of most treatment programs for pathological gambling is total abstinence from gambling. This goal is a further indication of the conceptual and organizational resemblance between AA and GA. It is common in each group respectively to speak of the "recovering alcoholic" or the "recovering pathological gambler," but never "recovered." Both groups invoke a particular version of the disease model which dictates that once stricken, never cured. Even the National Council on Problem Gambling's motto, "Compulsive gambling is a treatable disorder," does not include the additional notion of *cure* (National Council on Problem Gambling [NCPG], 1989).

TABLE 1: TWENTY QUESTIONS ABOUT GAMBLING BEHAVIOR*

1. Did you ever lose time from work due to gambling?
2. Has gambling ever made your home life unhappy?
3. Did gambling affect your reputation?
4. Have you ever felt remorse after gambling?
5. Did you ever gamble to get money with which to pay debts or otherwise solve financial difficulties?
6. Did gambling cause a decrease in your ambition or efficiency?
7. After losing did you feel you must return as soon as possible and win back your losses?
8. After a win did you have a strong urge to return and win more?
9. Did you often gamble until your last dollar was gone?
10. Did you ever borrow to finance your gambling?
11. Have you ever sold anything to finance gambling?
12. Were you reluctant to use "gambling money" for normal expenditures?
13. Did gambling make you careless of the welfare of yourself and your family?
14. Did you ever gamble longer than you had planned?
15. Have you ever gambled to escape worry or trouble?
16. Have you ever committed, or considered committing an illegal act to finance gambling?
17. Did gambling cause you to have difficulty in sleeping?
18. Do arguments, disappointments or frustrations create within you an urge to gamble?
19. Did you ever have an urge to celebrate any good fortune by a few hours of gambling?
20. Have you ever considered self destruction as a result of your gambling?

*Note: From *Twenty Questions* by Gamblers Anonymous, 1980, Los Angeles, CA: Gamblers Anonymous. Copyright ©1980 by Gamblers Anonymous.

Inpatient and residential rehabilitation treatment programs generally reflect this underlying assumption of the chronic and incurable nature of pathological gambling. In these programs, counseling and group therapy are used to develop what they maintain is necessary insight in the pathological gambler about the ongoing risk of remission and to support the recovering gambler's resolve to live the rest of his or her life without gambling (Lesieur, 1979). Generally, participation in group therapy means a mixture of attendance at GA meetings and participation in other group sessions led by a trained counselor (Greenberg, 1980). Regular participation at GA meetings is usually considered to be the most significant step a pathological gambler can take in the process of recovery (Custer, 1986) because GA members are considered, by GA at least, to be the "true experts" in helping pathological gamblers in the recovery process (Allcock & Dickerson, 1986; Brown, 1986; Lesieur & Custer, 1984; Martinez, 1983).

Advocates of the treatment goal of total abstinence have had almost exclusive control over the formulation of policy and treatment goals for all public-sponsored treatment programs for pathological gamblers in the United States (Rosecrance, 1985). This dominance has been granted to these advocates because of the general acceptance of GA's other major foundational argument that pathological gambling is a disease. The uncritical conceptualization of pathological gambling as a disease with primarily biological causation rather than as a behavioral disorder resulting from a complex process of behavioral conditioning and/or psychological conflict has thus far resulted in most inpatient and residential treatment being managed under a medical model of care and decision-making authority. The bias of the disease model has been criticized for limiting the range of treatment and research on pathological gambling (Rosecrance, 1989). Debate over both the validity and utility of the disease model of gambling and the related medical model of treatment has been waged with the same level of intensity and lack of rational resolution as has been true in the field of alcohol and drug abuse (Abt & McGurrin, 1989; Blume, 1988; Dickerson, 1988; Peele, 1984; Taber, 1988). A critical review of the literature on the comparative analysis of gambling as a disease versus a behavioral disorder is beyond the scope of this guide, but it is important for the practicing clinician to realize that this debate remains a volatile issue and has very strong implications for treatment programs and techniques.

The overall effectiveness of treatment focused exclusively, or even primarily, on total abstinence has definite limitations and may even be counterproductive to the effective treatment of problem gamblers (Scodel, 1964). Although GA's use of the term disease implies a rather uniform causal dynamic underlying pathological gambling, there is already a sufficient body of clinical and research data to suggest that any single cause and single treatment is naïve and excessively simplistic.

The emphasis on uninterrupted abstinence as the primary indication of treatment success can actually backfire when pathological gamblers experience episodic relapse into gambling activity. Although attendance at GA meetings often provides sufficient peer support to achieve temporary remission, the recurrence of gambling activity is fairly common and may lead recovering gamblers into self-defeating gambling binges because they feel they will never succeed in sustained abstinence. Rather than attempting to control their gambling during these relapses, they seem to prefer instead "the voluptuousness of giving oneself up for lost" (Halliday & Fuller, 1974, p. 24). Several investigators have reported on the high dropout rate from GA (Ashton, 1979; Brown, 1984, 1986; Lester, 1980; Moody, 1972; Preston & Smith, 1985). Additionally the fact is that some categories of persons such as women, racial minorities, and adolescents usually do not even join GA because they feel uncomfortable about their underrepresentation (Brown, 1986).

Controlled Gambling. The alternative to total abstinence and life-long involvement in GA is generally referred to as *controlled gambling*. Like its counterpart in the treatment of alcohol abuse, *controlled drinking*, it represents a minority position and is generally criticized more as ideological heresy than an alternative treatment approach that should be evaluated scientifically (Peele, 1984; Rosecrance, 1989). One of the primary supporters of treatment designed to develop a capacity for controlled gambling has been John Rosecrance. He has based his own approach on work done outside the United States where both controlled drinking and controlled gambling have enjoyed more widespread and objective reception among treatment and research professionals. Specifically, he cites the British and Australian successes in controlled gambling programs as reported by Oldman (1974, 1978), Rankin (1982), and Allcock and Dickerson (1986). The Australian reports are especially noteworthy because controlled gambling has been part of comprehensive treatment programs for over 5 years.

Rosecrance's central argument for treatment goal alternatives to abstinence is that

> current treatment programs by demanding abstinence often cause delays in seeking treatment (Lester, 1980)

since troubled gamblers are reluctant to permanently give up an activity that serves as an important source of excitement and camaraderie in their lives. At present, gamblers assume that if they want treatment they must first agree to give up gambling (Martinez, 1975). Therefore, only desperate losers are willing to seek help. It seems wasteful to discourage all but the most severely troubled from seeking assistance. Controlled programs, by offering an alternative approach, are capable of reaching gamblers who have not yet hit "rock bottom" but who nevertheless are experiencing serious problems related to gambling. (Rosecrance, 1989, p. 156)

Following Oldman's model of problem gambling (1978), Rosecrance virtually rejects the concept of *pathological* gambling and any underlying uncontrollable impulse to gamble and argues that problem gambling results from inappropriate gambling strategies rather than psychological disorders. The proper response to correct this problem is to educate so-called pathological gamblers to utilize more appropriate strategies in their gambling activity. This never happens in the current conventional gambling treatment programs in the United States because treatment staff not only reject the basic concept of controlled gambling, but also because of:

1. Lack of knowledge concerning appropriate gaming strategies and/or money management.
2. An inability to develop empathy for gamblers who want to maintain participation in an ongoing treatment program while continuing to gamble.
3. The fact that inappropriate strategies are manifested outside of a counseling setting.
4. Failure to be aware of sources that could aid gamblers in developing appropriate strategies. (Rosecrance, 1989, p. 152)

Rosecrance has provided a general description of the basic components of a controlled gambling rehabilitation program but has not yet reported or made available a fully detailed program manual that can be used for establishing such a program. Basically, the staff includes some mental health professionals such as psychologists, psychiatrists, or psychiatric social workers. The core counselors, however, are active gamblers who are able to provide empathic understanding of the problem gambler's plight and also can provide objective and technically informed evaluation and correction of the problem gambler's inappropriate gambling strategies. The mutual understanding of the gambling experience that exists between this peer counselor and client supposedly allows them to relate on both a cognitive and affective level. Problem gamblers are highly motivated to learn new strategies and modify their gambling behavior because the peer counselor is not focused on extinguishing gambling activity, but instead is perceived by clients as a knowledgeable compatriot who is providing useful and relevant counsel that will allow clients to resolve a *gambling problem* without having to give up gambling. Rosecrance (1989) reports substantial success with at least one controlled gambling program that rehabilitated 50 clients who met the *DSM-III-R* criteria for pathological gambling. Certainly additional application and evaluation of this rehabilitation model is required before it can be reasonably appraised as an effective alternative to abstinence, but initial results suggest that it may be useful for at least some pathological gamblers.

Synoptic Model. Other less radical rehabilitation models have been proposed as alternatives to the orthodox disease model of pathological gambling with its requirements of total abstinence. These models are conceptually related to social learning theory and basic cybernetic or cognitive feedback principles (Abt et al., 1985; Brown, 1988; Ingram, 1985).

One example of these alternative models is Abt, McGurrin, and Smith's synoptic model (1985). This model regards pathological gambling as the outcome of the gamblers' failure to integrate the norms of the gambling situation with their own motivations and to use feedback provided in the actual gambling situation to correct their increasingly problematic behavior. Gambling is conceptualized as social behavior that achieves meaning by reference to the contexts in which it occurs. For example, the apparently objective monetary costs and benefits of gambling are often regarded within the reference frame of gambling as symbols of the gambler's willingness to sacrifice in order to achieve the ecstasy and release of "the action." Judgments about the irrationality of betting in the face of unfavorable odds may be very incomplete without also calculating the other rewards which the gambler achieves simply by participating in the process of gambling. Gamblers play under many different conditions and for many different reasons. The synoptic model focuses, therefore, on a gambler's evaluation of the meaning of gaming activities within a social context. It regards the gambler's information processing activity as the principal mechanism that integrates societal (macro level) and individual (micro level) causes of gambling behavior.

The synoptic model represents the gambler's reality with eight interrelated sets of variables (see Figure 1, p. 43).

The macro level of the gambler's social reality consists of

1. status variables such as socioeconomic status, marital status, and disposable time and income;
2. situational variables such as opportunity to gamble and number of gambling colleagues;
3. contextual variables such as local gambling regulations and statutes;
4. social transformation rules which are the social norms that define the general values and conduct of the gambling environment; and
5. gambling event variables such as type of equipment and odds.

The micro level consists of

6. psychological variables such as self-esteem, personality disorder, and locus of control;
7. the gambling action such as actual gambling styles and strategies; and
8. social feedback signal variables such as peer approval and perceived cost/benefit outcomes after a series of wagers.

The application of the macro and micro level transformation rules by gamblers in a particular situation is the means by which gamblers produce a framework of meaning to evaluate the degree to which their conduct and its consequences are validating their self-image as a successful gambler. For example, if a gambler receives feedback that he or she is being a *poor loser*, this will also signal that he or she is a poor gambler, because manifest discontent about losing is a deviation from the universal gambling norm that calls for stoic acceptance of loss as an integral part of the action. Accepting random losses gracefully shows character and style which is itself a basis for winning respect from fellow gamblers. As with many other forms of social behavior, unfa-

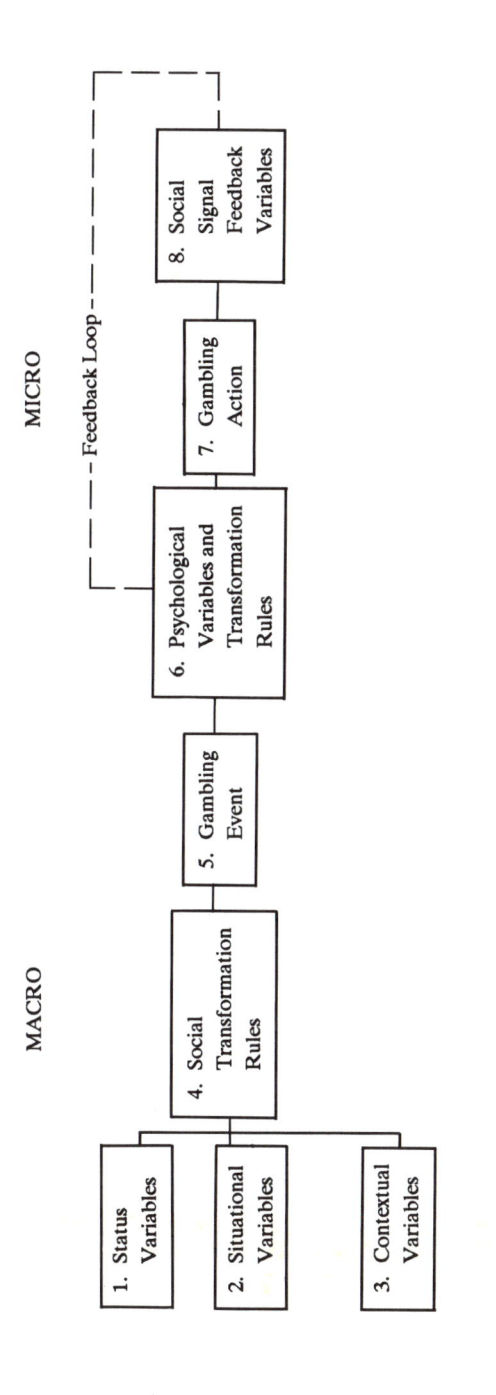

Figure 1. A synoptic model of gambling behavior.

vorable peer evaluation based on the gambler's failure to *play by the rules* may be experienced as a far greater loss than a financial loss on a series of gaming outcomes. In the long run, a gambler's sense of success or failure at gambling usually depends on an interrelated set of variables and not just on calculated financial gains or losses as may be the case for nongamblers.

McGurrin (1989) has developed some treatment applications of the synoptic model. One of these applications can be demonstrated by continuing with the example of the *poor loser, poor gambler* situation. Because many pathological gamblers are found to have low self-esteem and are very reactive to the judgment of fellow gamblers, the therapist should first assess the particular client's level of self-esteem and sensitivity to issues of self-worth. If the client has low self-esteem, the therapist hypothesizes that the client's practice of escalating bets after losses is not only a method of attempting to recover financial loss, but also and especially a means of accentuating the gambler's style of remaining cool and unthreatened in the face of recurring lost bets. The therapist then employs a simulated gambling situation with the client in which the client is allowed to increase amounts bet in response to losses but is given feedback by the therapist that a strategy that increases risk of further losses suggests a loss of control and indicates panic in the client. The therapist then substitutes the feedback of reduced approval of gambling style with each loss. After a series of five or six such bets and feedback messages, the therapist involves the client in discussion about motives for increasing the amount of money bet in each play of the game. The therapist points out that the client would have just as likely gained respect from other gamblers if the client had accepted his or her losses and not tried to recover large amounts on a single bet. The therapist also suggests that the client could have quit at any time and resumed betting at some other time. This decision to stop gambling temporarily could be viewed by others as a sign of good gambling judgment worthy of respect. This exercise is repeated at least several times depending on how responsive the client is and how much insight seems to develop each time it is carried out.

In a second example of synoptic applications, the therapist informs the client that he or she will be required to guess the numeric identity of a card drawn from the top of a set of five ordinary numbered playing cards. After the therapist shuffles the cards, the client is asked to identify the top card and the therapist then reveals the card's numeric identity. Let us assume that the

Pathological Gambling

client correctly guesses the card's numeric identity on the first shuffle. Whenever the card is correctly identified, the client is asked to read aloud the following printed message provided by the therapist:

> I have just correctly identified the top card before you turned it over. That is not easy to do and you and I know it. I like the feeling I get from winning at games of chance. Let us try it again to see whether I guess it right or wrong.

After the client reads the message, the therapist reshuffles the cards and asks the client to guess the top card. This continues until the client incorrectly guesses the card's identity.

Whenever the client guesses the card's identity incorrectly twice in a row, the client is asked to read aloud the following printed message provided by the therapist:

> I have just incorrectly identified the card twice in a row. I do not know why I should continue guessing if I am losing. If I were betting money, I would be losing money also. Usually when I lose, I lose money and I lose the feeling of excitement from winning.

After the client reads the message, the therapist asks the client to explain what is wrong with the message. The dialogue typically takes the following form:

Therapist: Tell me what is wrong with that message you just read.
Client: Nothing, I guess. You know it makes sense.
Therapist: No, tell me what is wrong with it.
Client: What? I don't know.
Therapist: Yes you know, you said the message makes sense, but you don't act that way. Don't you make sense?
Client: Oh, you mean my compulsive gambling?
Therapist: Yes, what makes it different from the message?

The therapist keeps directing discussions about discrepancies between the message and the client's acknowledged gambling behavior by requesting that the client explain his or her motivation for continuing the discrepancies when the client gambles. The therapist concludes each such discussion by emphasizing that normal gamblers set an early limit on continuing losses and win other people's respect for doing so. The card selecting, message reading, and related feedback discussion are repeated several times in a session.

Applications such as the two examples just presented are included in as many sessions as the therapist judges to be useful in assisting the client to recognize and utilize corrective feedback regarding problematic gambling behavior. The therapist should anticipate that many clients will experience these applications as simplistic and artificial compared to actual gambling situations. The client should be told at the outset that the primary purpose of the application is to enhance the client's use of feedback rather than providing a gambling opportunity.

The synoptic feedback approach provides a means by which the therapist becomes a relevant source of information and influence in changing the client's gambling behavior without totally separating the client from gambling through required abstinence. The synoptic technique is not used as a total replacement for other aspects of therapeutic intervention with the pathological gambler, but is intended as a supplemental approach in cases where controlled gambling is a tentatively accepted treatment goal. More conventional techniques that focus on affective issues and family dynamics should also be included in the treatment plan.

The synoptic technique has not been used with any pathological gamblers during inpatient rehabilitation. It has been found to be partially successful with some pathological gamblers who entered outpatient therapy without any previous inpatient care, and with some pathological gamblers who had inpatient care but did not sustain abstinence during aftercare outpatient therapy (McGurrin, 1986). There is currently insufficient data to reliably evaluate the long-range (i.e., 10 years) effectiveness of the controlled gambling and synoptic model techniques in treating pathological gamblers. These techniques may be limited in effectiveness to pathological gamblers who have not yet lost complete control over the impulse to gamble. They are available, however, to all persons who need to modify their gambling activity and would participate in treatment so long as it does not require abstinence. There are a substantial number of problem and pathological gamblers to whom this condition applies.

INPATIENT TREATMENT

The majority of pathological gamblers begin treatment in specialized inpatient programs because they have denied the need for treatment until major life disruptions have seriously affected their personal, marital, and vocational functioning and financial status. Typically, there will be a crisis that involves several of these areas simultaneously. By this point, gamblers may already have experienced several months of increasingly intense and frequent anxiety attacks, periods of insomnia, and recurrent alternation between manic and depressed affect. They recognize the developing crises in their life and understand their inability to continue avoiding or escaping the consequences of their gambling activity. Gamblers may also report dissociative-like experiences or feelings of derealization that create great difficulty in concentrating and completing routine tasks (Kuley & Jacobs, 1988). Thoughts of suicide, or even threats of suicide to family members and friends, are fairly common at this point.

The most widely accepted model of the natural course of pathological gambling has been developed by Custer. This model, presented in Figure 2 (p. 48), represents the development of pathological gambling disorder as a passage through sequential phases of loss of control over gambling and increasing personal and social problems related to gambling. A final "hitting bottom" phase occurs when the gambler's life is in general crisis and often warrants inpatient treatment.

Inpatient admission based on a primary diagnosis of pathological gambling is rare because of the difficulty in acquiring private health insurers' preapproval of payment for inpatient care of an individual with this diagnosis. Because the gambler at this point of crisis is usually suffering from acute anxiety, depression, and suicidal ideation, and may have been abusing alcohol or drugs sufficiently to require detoxification, the more typical admitting diagnosis is appropriately one of the several Mood Disorders (*DSM-III-R*, 296, 300, 301, or 311) or Psychoactive Substance Use Disorders (303-305). At private hospitals with specific programs for treatment of pathological gamblers, the gambler and a family member are often interviewed separately by telephone in advance of actual admission to determine if the gambler can be admitted under an appropriate diagnosis. If accepted, the gambler is then evaluated and assigned an official diagnosis by a staff psychiatrist as a part of the official admission process.

Pathological Gambling

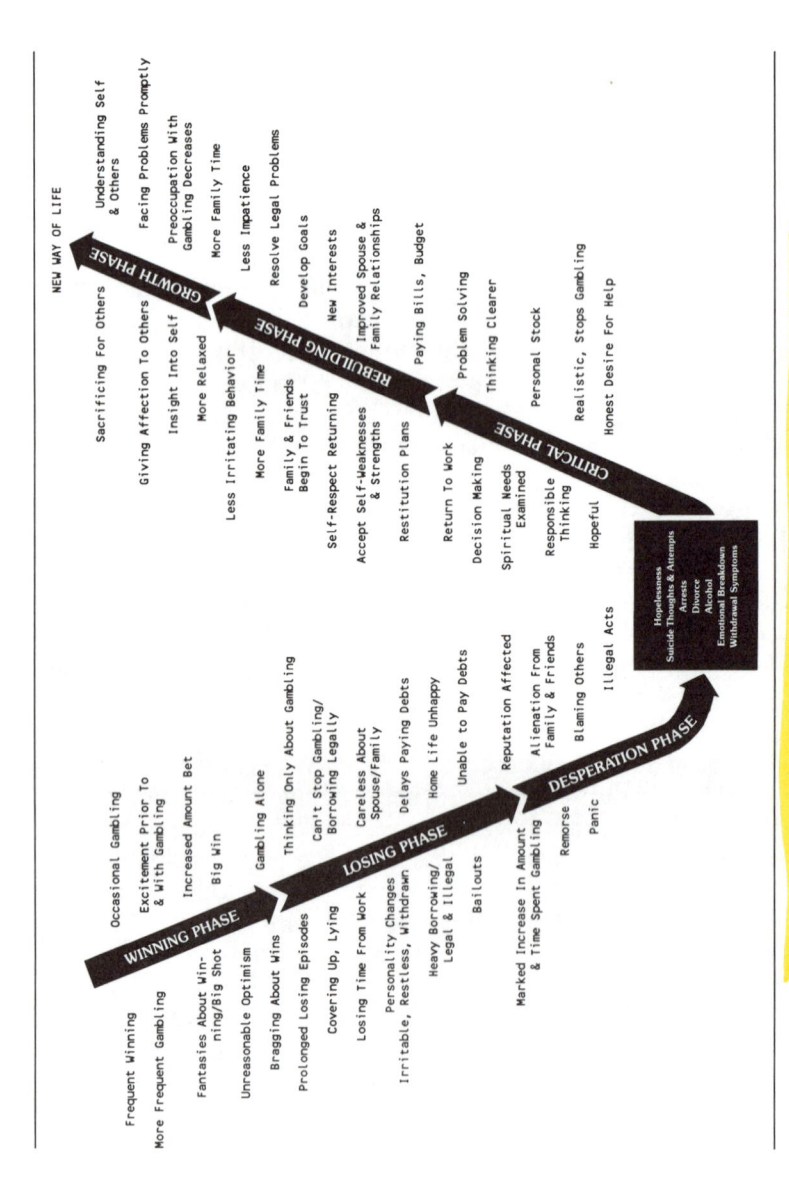

Figure 2. The progression of compulsive gambling and recovery.

48

Most formal inpatient and rehabilitation programs are 20 to 30 days in length and have a treatment cost ranging from $20,000 to $28,000. Patients typically receive basic medical, psychiatric, and psychological assessments preliminary to the assignment to a treatment team and development of a treatment plan. Treatment teams usually consist of a staff psychiatrist, a primary therapist or counselor, and a social worker who coordinates and acts as a liaison to family, employers, and other significant persons who are outside of the hospital. Primary therapists or counselors are often master's level psychologists, MSWs, psychiatric nurses, or addiction counselors.

Treatment objectives during the first week generally involve stabilizing the patient emotionally, selecting and monitoring medications if indicated, and orienting the patient to hospital and treatment program regulations. Patients are required to follow highly structured schedules of daily activity which can include prohibiting all contact with family members or others outside of the hospital until the treatment team allows such contact. Telephone use is a scheduled and closely monitored privilege during most of the treatment program. This enforced, detention-like atmosphere is maintained to prohibit access to alcohol, drugs, or the opportunity to place bets or gamble. The total abstinence from addictive substances and behavior is a control goal of most treatment programs, and is usually a requirement for being allowed to remain in the program.

By the middle of the first week, the patient is involved in group therapy sessions. These focus on reducing the patients' denial of their inability to gamble in a normal, controlled manner. It is important for them to recognize that what they had believed were their own private techniques for beating the odds in gambling are essentially the same unsuccessful techniques employed by the other pathological gamblers in the group. Groups often include a volunteer who is a recovering gambler as a means of introducing the patient to the concept of peer counseling or sponsorship on the part of GA (Franklin & Ciarrocchi, 1987).

There is usually a strong educational component introduced into treatment by the second week. Patients are required to attend sessions in which they are counseled on personal finances and money management. Often they must develop a time schedule for paying back the debts incurred through gambling. It is thought to be very important that the patient accept responsibility for paying back debts without financial assistance from family or friends. This requirement not only confronts patients with issues they will encounter after they have left the hospital, but also discourages resumption of co-dependent relationships with family members, which have been interrupted by inpatient treatment.

During the first 2 weeks of treatment, family members are seen collaterally by a member of the treatment team. The goals of these sessions are to (a) educate them on the disorder of pathological gambling, (b) inform them about the goals of the patient's treatment plan, (c) allow the treatment team member to develop impressions of the family's dynamics, and (d) provide initial supportive therapy to family members (especially the spouse) who may be dealing with mixed feelings of resentment, guilt, and neglect in the face of all the attention and support that is being directed toward the patient.

By the third week, many programs include spouses and, sometimes, other key family members, in group sessions. This allows both patients and family members to recognize the common features of pathological gambling that have affected other patients and their families. Pathological gambling, as with other pathological behavior, is typically the "great family secret" that family members do not discuss and that they collectively deny. Sessions involving patients and family members are very useful in teaching families to acknowledge the problem gambling and discuss it in a healthy and constructive manner. These sessions also encourage the emotional expression that has often been avoided by the family. The therapist can offer assurance that such expression may benefit them, that they will not be allowed to exceed the limits of the therapeutic situation, and that, over time, they can integrate the material in a meaningful way.

Many inpatient programs schedule GA meetings in the hospital several evenings a week. This allows patients to begin attending meetings as well as to have further contact with peer counselors. It also helps develop the practice of attending meetings which will be important to patients after their release.

OUTPATIENT TREATMENT

Outpatient therapy may begin under either of two different conditions. First, and most common, the client has recently completed an inpatient rehabilitation program and has been referred to an independent outpatient therapist as a part of the aftercare plan. Usually the client also will have been enrolled in a GA group. The client is typically motivated to attend at least several outpatient sessions because therapy is accepted as a continuation of the inpatient program. The client's spouse and family usually have been counseled by the inpatient treatment team leader to expect and support follow-up psychotherapy after the pathological gambler has been discharged from inpatient treatment.

The client's GA sponsor also may encourage the client to participate in outpatient therapy depending on the attitude of the sponsor and the particular GA group. GA's ideology on pathological gambling often has no practical significance for the independent psychotherapist and treatment techniques. There are times, however, when GA's somewhat evangelical themes (public confession before peers, recovery of self-worth through self-criticism and abstinence, dealing with life only one day at a time, and achieving a vaguely defined form of spiritual redemption through surrender to a greater power) may create conflict with the goals of a particular outpatient treatment plan.

The second condition for beginning outpatient psychotherapy occurs without the client having "hit bottom" and gone through hospital care. This client is often threatened with divorce, loss of employment, or other conditions if he or she does not become involved in therapy. Usually such an individual is not strongly self-motivated to seek help. Strong denials that gambling is out of control usually exist. Typically, the client is extremely cordial and cooperative, expressing a somewhat patronizing and indulgent attitude toward family members who have communicated concern, as well as toward the psychotherapist. The opportunity to demonstrate a basic control over the therapy situation by skillfully conducting a hustle of all parties involved becomes a welcomed challenge to the client. During the early sessions, a self-imposed but limited period of abstinence from gambling is often volunteered by the client to demonstrate capacity for control. The client entering outpatient therapy under this second condition is usually far more difficult to work with, at least initially.

Miller's (1986) Four-Phase Approach utilizes a four-phase individual outpatient treatment technique that views recovery from pathological gambling as a process whereby the pathological gambler chooses to lose an addiction to gambling, while mourning the loss of the gambling as one would any severe loss. Miller's model is a very useful generic approach to outpatient psychotherapy for the pathological gambler even if the therapist chooses not to include the additional assumptions of a parallel between discontinuing gambling and the experience of grief and mourning a severe loss.

Phase one of this approach focuses on inducing gamblers to commit themselves to abstinence. It is crucial at this phase for the therapist to confront the gambler's denial and minimization of his or her inability to control gambling behavior. At the same time, it is important that the therapist not become manipulative or too adversarial because of the risk of the client's premature withdrawal from therapy. The therapist must be authentic, involved, and supportive, but also firm on the issue of abstinence. Anxiety must be managed carefully so that clients remain motivated to change, but not so overwhelmed by anxiety related to discontinuing gambling that treatment is terminated or gambling behaviors return.

In the second phase, the client must be enabled to identify and confront the problems that have been caused by gambling. Continued abstinence is important and the therapist should support the client's ability to cope with the increasing distress resulting from abstinence. The focus of sessions will often be on managing urges and thoughts about gambling. Engagement is a difficult but crucial issue at this phase. Most pathological gamblers have been so dishonest and manipulative with other people that an honest and open emotional relationship with the therapist may be difficult to develop initially.

The third phase focuses on longer term problems. Developing greater internal control over behavior and accepting greater intimacy in relationships, with more direct and expressive recognition of feelings of anger, sadness, and guilt related to gambling, become important issues in this phase. Sufficient structure and direction by the therapist must be maintained to prevent regression.

In the fourth phase, therapy is less structured and similar in process to open-ended, client-centered therapies. The client should be able to tolerate increasing amounts of anxiety and acknowledge his or her personal limitations in controlling gambling.

Other Approaches. A variety of different models of outpatient psychotherapy have been utilized over the past 20 years in treating pathological gambling. Bolen and Boyd (1968) describe successful results with couple's group therapy with treatment lasting about 1 year. They claim that there was typically a reduction of chronic anxiety, depression, and destructive criticism within couples. The couples also developed more effective defense techniques, became more spontaneous and authentic in interpersonal relations, and assumed more responsible and appropriate marital roles.

Goorney (1968), Barker (1968), and Seagar (1970) report limited success with aversion therapy. Tepperman (1985) reports substantive success using short-term (12 weeks) conjoint group therapy using the Gamblers Anonymous 12-Step program materials as topics of group discussion. Each session began with one or more members reading aloud one of the steps and then group members each discussing the meaning the step had for their respective lives.

ROLE OF FAMILY IN CAUSE AND TREATMENT OF PATHOLOGICAL GAMBLING

The significance of family dynamics in treating and explaining pathological gambling has received increasing attention since about 1970 (Franklin & Thomas, 1989; Jacobs, 1989). The initial recognition of the importance of providing some support to the gambler's family was prompted by GA's further imitation of the basic AA model, which includes Al-Anon, a support group for alcoholics' families. In 1960, the first Gam-Anon groups were formed, although there were no support techniques specific to the issue of pathological gambling that distinguished Gam-Anon from Al-Anon. Even today, the basic focus of Gam-Anon is to separate the family members from feelings of guilt, responsibility, and other inappropriate emotional reactions toward the pathological gambler's gambling activity. The problem of codependency and enabling the addict seem apparent in many relationships between pathological gamblers and their family members regarding the different ways in which they may be influencing the gambler's behavior without either party consciously realizing the nature of the involvement.

The intentional inclusion of the pathological gambler's family in professional mental health treatment lagged behind the peer support group approach substantially. Custer's innovative treatment program for pathological gambling at the Brecksville, Ohio, Veterans Administration Hospital did recognize the significance of the family in the recovery process, but the inpatient structure of the program greatly limited opportunity for family member involvement. Furthermore, because the first several programs were provided through the Veterans Administration Hospitals, access to these programs for both the gambler and family was limited to veterans.

The first treatment program for pathological gamblers that was open to the general public was offered by Taylor Manor Hospital in Elliot City, Maryland, in 1979. Both the inpatient and aftercare portions of their program placed increasing attention on the gambler's family. By 1982, New York State funded outpatient programs at St. Vincent's North Richmond Community Mental Health Center on Staten Island and the Rochester Health Association in Rochester, New York. Subsequent increased state funding for outpatient programs for pathological gamblers has expanded services to Queens, Manhattan, and Buffalo, New York. Other states which have provided some funding for outpatient programs are Nevada, Massachusetts, New Jersey, Iowa, and Connecticut. Currently there are approximately 45 formal treatment programs for pathological gamblers and their families nationally (Franklin & Thoms, 1989).

FAMILY OF ORIGIN

Although most interest in the significance of family dynamics for explaining and treating pathological gambling has focused on the conjugal family in which the gambler participates as an adult spouse and parent, there has been limited interest in the gambler's family of origin where the formative experiences of infancy, childhood, and adolescence occurred. This relative lack of interest in the etiological significance of pathological gamblers' experiences within their families of origin may be a reflection of two assumptions about pathological gambling that have recently been challenged conceptually and empirically. First, until Jacobs' recent research documenting the extent of late childhood and early adolescent gambling activity (1989), it was generally assumed that pathological gambling was an adult phenomenon. Clearly, this assumption is no longer valid because of the increasing research findings that document childhood and adolescent gambling for money on sports and other types of games of chance previously thought to be restricted to adults.

Second, the primary sources of influence to gamble were related to persons and events that existed outside of the family of origin and did not become effective until the gambler became a young adult and separated from the family of origin. Recent data have shown, however, that approximately 40% of adult pathological gamblers first gambled in the company of an adult family member or older sibling, and approximately 45% came from families in which one or both parents were active gamblers (Franklin & Ciarrocchi, 1987; McGurrin, 1986). These data suggest that positive values and attitudes toward gambling as well as opportunity to learn gambling behavior may begin within the gambler's family of origin. Furthermore, Strachan (1989) reports that women pathological gamblers tend to have had very dysfunctional families of origin. Forty-two percent had an alcoholic parent or were from an alcoholic family. Forty-two percent had parents who gambled excessively. Thirty-three percent reported being physically abused by their parents, and 29% claimed that they had been sexually abused as children.

The importance of knowing more about the experience of pathological gamblers within their family of origin becomes increasingly apparent as knowledge of gambling phenomena in general increases. Certainly the literature on the etiology and treatment of personality disorders could provide a fruitful basis for designing further research on the significance of early childhood experiences in the development of pathological gambling, because, at least conceptually, personality disorders and pathological gambling have been linked (Rosenthal, 1986). The limited amount of formal research and even published clinical case analyses on the issue of the causal role of family of origin and pathological gambling is a serious shortcoming in the analysis of pathological gambling. Clinicians and research scientists should both be encouraged to investigate and report on this aspect of pathological gambling.

CONJUGAL FAMILY

As an adult, the pathological gambler's family roles are often those of spouse and parent. Since demographic studies have reported such a disproportionate number of male pathological gamblers, the majority of family studies have viewed the effects of pathological gambling on wife, mother, and children. More recent research has revealed, however, that as many as a third of pathological gamblers are female and many are married. Research on the female pathological gambler as wife and mother is very much needed to expand our knowledge of the effects of pathological gambling on family life.

Effects on Spouse. The tensions between the gambler and spouse develop over time and have been classified into stages of worsening symptoms and progressive decline in the marriage (Franklin & Thoms, 1989; Wexler, 1984). The first phase is characterized by one spouse's early realization of the other spouse's gambling problem combined with an attempt to deny its significance. The wife usually keeps her concern to herself, considers her husband's gambling activity as a passing interest, and is easily reassured by the gambler that he is in control of his gambling. In fact, at this stage the gambler is often successful in concealing the extent of his gambling and the wife tacitly agrees not to create tension by confronting the gambler with her concerns about the possible problems related to continued gambling.

The transition into the second phase begins when unpaid bills and financial crises can no longer be denied by the wife. She experiences increasing rejection by the gambler and accusations of harassment and spousal disloyalty. The wife also attempts to control the consequences of the gambling by arranging partial loans from friends and relatives. This strategy simply enables the pathological gambler to continue gambling and results in isolating the wife from her own support system of friends and relatives because she ignores their advice to leave the gambler to face the legal consequences of debt on his own. The combination of rejection and isolation often leads to early stages of depression for the wife.

In the second phase, the continued gambling and worsening financial condition increase the wife's efforts to arrange bailouts and to make excuses to creditors, family, friends, and others affected by the gambler's debt and continued gambling. If the gambler and spouse are parents, the mother must now provide explanations to the children about their father's increasing absence and uncaring behavior. The children begin to experience both emotional and material deprivation because of the gambling problems. The spouse begins to be emotionally and physically exhausted by her unsuccessful efforts to control the gambler's activity and to forestall financial foreclosure. She experiences episodes of acute anxiety, confusion, and resentment followed by extended periods of depression.

In the third phase, the spouse experiences the undeniable realization that she cannot control her husband's gambling, nor can she protect herself and her children from its manifold adverse consequences. She may alternate between panic and rage.

Shortly thereafter, she enters a fourth phase which is the spouse's version of "hitting bottom." In her own feelings of extreme hopelessness, she may begin abusing alcohol or prescription medications. She often begins preparation for divorce and may even consider suicide. There is a strong sense of hopelessness and loss of control over life.

Effects on Children. The effects of pathological gambling on the gambler's children are quite similar to those observed in many dysfunctional families, especially the alcoholic's family. The children respond to pressures from both parents, and many children experience severe role conflicts. As family tensions increase from the progressively worsening gambling, children may become scapegoats, peacemakers, or strive to replace the failing parents by becoming the overresponsible children who try desperately to restore order to the deteriorating family environment. Often with their own feelings of anxiety, anger, and depression, these children assume responsibility for the emotional tensions of the family. Unable to reduce the family's conflicting emotions, these children inevitably begin acting out. Several common ways are through inconsistent academic performance with under- or overachieving, substance abuse, and even gambling activity (Franklin & Thoms, 1989). Jacobs' (1989) research on children of pathological gamblers has revealed consistently a higher propensity for use of tobacco, alcohol, and a range of narcotics than their classroom peers with average parents. These children also had an earlier age of onset for behaviors such as gorging food and gambling activity. In fact, "children of problem gamblers showed what may be inferred to be a greater drive state to escape reality and a greater propensity for seeking mood-elevating substances and stimulating experiences than did their peers with average parents" (Jacobs, 1989, p. 276).

The family environment may have a variety of related interpersonal tensions, all of which create a progressively stressful environment for the children's psychosocial development. Frequent disappointments result from unkept promises by the gambling parent who finds it easier to make promises for shared activity than to keep them. The children's repeated experience of abused trust in the parent inculcates psychosocial defenses which protect the child from psychic pain while also tending to excuse the parent's behavior. In fact, the child's fear of being abandoned by the gambling parent may actually motivate him or her to excessive efforts to please this parent in return for any possible approval or love from the parent. Herein lies the basis of the dynamics of the "enabling" child who protects and excuses the parent's problematic behavior. Children may also experience severe conflict when solicited by the mother into alliances of mutual protection from the bad father. Children and mother begin to look to each other for emotional security and satisfaction which should be provided to them respectively by a mature adult male filling the roles of husband and father. The substitute alliance often generates feelings of guilt and shame among the children and mother. They feel an uneasy sense of disloyalty to the pathological gambler who may occasionally rebuke the family for locking him out of their lives.

These children are also unusually sensitive about relationships with persons outside of the family. The family usually attempts to conceal the "shameful" problem of the gambler and consequently remains very guarded about how close to allow friends and neighbors to approach them in relationships in which the family's secret might be at risk of disclosure. Table 2 (p. 59) lists many of the characteristics that frequently appear in the personality profile of children of pathological gamblers.

FORENSIC ISSUES

Increasingly psychologists and psychiatrists are being engaged by defense lawyers and the judicial system to conduct psychological and diagnostic evaluations of persons whose gambling activity is seen as a relevant and potentially mitigating factor in evaluating their degree of responsibility for a criminal act. Although a diagnosis of pathological gambling presently does not constitute the basis of a legal defense, it may be allowed as a part of testimony and as a consideration in determining sentence in the event of a conviction. It is useful, therefore, for clinicians to have at least a general knowledge of the forensic aspects of pathological gambling. Milton Earl Burglass has published an excellent report on this issue (Burglass, 1989); the structure and content of this section have been heavily influenced by Burglass' work.

There are two basic issues that determine the legal relevance of testimony on pathological gambling. First is that of the mental or "insanity" defense in criminal prosecution. Judicial opinion on a legal defense based on the defendant's mental condition at the time of the criminal act has changed many times since the classic M'Naghten rule established in 1843. Under this rule, ordinary legal responsibility was excused if it could be established that the defendant could not distinguish between right and wrong because of mental disease affect or disorder at the time the offense was committed.

TABLE 2: PSYCHOLOGICAL PROBLEMS AND CHARACTERISTICS COMMON AMONG PATHOLOGICAL GAMBLERS' SPOUSES AND CHILDREN

FEMALE SPOUSE:

1. Co-dependent and enabler to pathological gambler
2. Passive-aggressive orientation toward social power
3. Poor self-image, low self-esteem
4. Difficulty expressing anger and assigning blame to others
5. Excessively focused on the needs of husband and children
6. Increasing anger, anxiety, and depression over time
7. Increasingly socially isolated
8. Inappropriately protective of husband and children
9. Uses self-denial and personal sacrifice to instill guilt and obligation in family members
10. Delays acknowledging seriousness of husband's gambling

CHILDREN:

1. Inappropriately assume responsibility for father's pathological gambling and family tensions
2. Excessively attempt to please father
3. Inappropriately attempt to protect mother from father's criticism or other abuse
4. Overachievement and excessive achievement anxiety
5. Chronic feeling of social embarrassment and discomfort
6. Fear of abandonment or betrayal by close associates and authority figures
7. Denial and repression of anger until episodic rage responses release emotion
8. Excessively loyal and protective of close associates
9. Chronically or episodically anxious and depressed
10. Somatasize anger
11. Expectant of disappointment, failure, and tragedy in life

---

This rule was later modified in several jurisdictions to include the condition in which the defendant was unable to control an impulse to commit a criminal act (*Smith v. United States*, 1929). Federal law has now come almost full circle in return to a

M'Naghten-type rule which requires that the defense prove that the defendant was unable to appreciate the nature and quality of the wrongfulness of the act. Even in a state or municipal statute where the defendant's capacity to conform his or her conduct to the requirement of the law is still considered, the insanity defense continues to be a difficult basis of argument because "the term 'voluntary' has defied any lasting and universally accepted definition. Most modern criminal codifications use adverbial qualifiers such as 'knowingly,' 'willfully,' or 'intentionally' to designate as voluntary an act performed consciously as a result of effort or determination" (Burglass, 1989, p. 206).

The second legal issue is the *exculpatory doctrine* in common law which allows the introduction into legal proceedings of evidence of specified mental conditions that may have significance in mitigation of culpability, liability, or responsibility for acts under consideration. The application of the principle of exculpatory rule requires the ability to demonstrate distinctions between general versus specific intent on the defendant's part, because culpability in some crimes requires demonstration of only general intent, while in others, demonstration of specific intent is required. These levels of discrimination are usually difficult to prove reliably in terms of current psychological methods and knowledge. Thus the rule of expert testimony by psychologist or psychiatrist in cases of impulse disorders such as pathological gambling remains problematic and subject to the judge's conditions of admissibility.

The primary reference case regarding the presentation of a defense based on pathological gambling is *United States v. Shorter* (1985). Shorter, the defendant, was charged with one count of tax evasion and six counts of willful failure to pay federal income taxes. The defense argued that Shorter's history of pathological gambling was a *direct* cause of his failure to pay his taxes. Their intention was to demonstrate through expert testimony that Shorter's compulsion to gamble rendered him incapable of making the decision to pay his taxes, thus establishing a lack of *willfulness* in his failure to pay his taxes. In this instance, *willfulness* is defined as "voluntary, intentional violation of a known legal duty" (*United States v. Pomponio*, 1976, p. 23).

Judge Greene, the trial court judge, determined the relevance of expert testimony on the relationship between pathological gambling and failure to pay taxes in this case by using a three-part test referred to as the Frye Test. The three points invoked under the Frye Test were the defense's ability to prove (a) that a disorder known as pathological gambling is recognized by the relevant community of experts; (b) that experts generally accept a causal link between pathological gambling and the failure to pay taxes; and (c) that the facts are sufficient to create a jury question as to whether the particular defendant suffers from a pathological gambling disorder (*United States v. Shorter*, 1985).

Following *United States v. Lewellyn* (1983), the judge ruled on the first point that pathological gambling is in fact recognized by the mental health community which constitutes a relevant community of experts for the disorder. On the second point, which required the defense to demonstrate that experts generally accept a causal link between pathological gambling and the failure to pay taxes, the judge heard testimony from seven expert witnesses. Defense experts emphasized different aspects of Shorter's disorder as it would affect willful failure to pay his taxes. One expert stated, for example, that a pathological gambler might choose not to pay taxes because of a belief that a "big win" from gambling is imminent and will then allow the gambler to pay off all financial obligations. A second defense expert stated that pathological gamblers lack the specific intent to commit the tax offense because they are irresistibly compelled to gamble with most of their money.

The prosecution introduced three forensic psychiatrists and a forensic psychologist as the government's expert witnesses. All three witnesses rejected unconditionally the contention that pathological gamblers are unable to make the decision to pay taxes because of the nature of their mental disorder. The Court as well pointed out that the mental health community does not sufficiently agree on a link between pathological gambling and criminal intent to support the relevance of pathological gambling with respect to an insanity defense for the crimes of robbery (*United States v. Gould*, 1984, p. 52); embezzlement (*United States v. Lewellyn*, 1983, p. 619); and interstate transportation of stolen goods (*United States v. Torniero*, 1984, pp. 732-734). Judge Greene agreed that there was insufficient agreement among the mental health community regarding a causal link between pathological gambling and failure to pay taxes and, therefore, rejected the defense request that expert testimony be admitted during the trial because the causal link condition of the Frye Test was not met.

Shorter was convicted on all seven charges and was sentenced to 40 months in prison and a $10,000 fine. Judge Greene's ruling on the application of the Frye Test regarding the issue of the admission of expert testimony was upheld on appeal (*United States v. Shorter*, 1987).

PRACTICAL ISSUES OF TREATMENT

Although Miller's (1986) model, discussed previously, presents one of the most complete approaches to the outpatient treatment of pathological gamblers, each clinician will discover particular practical concerns in the course of such treatment. Here, I would like to share my own hard-won practical recommendations for treating the pathological gambler:

1. Be assertive and directive with the client, but in an empathic way, as these individuals often attempt to take control of therapy sessions and direct discussions away from the problems they must resolve.
2. Establish with the client a reasonable balance between expectations for improvement and the likelihood of occasional regressions. Pathological gamblers often significantly underestimate the amount of time and effort that they must commit to therapy in order to resolve their problems.
3. Avoid discussions with clients about gambling. This topic is their specialty, and they usually know much more about it than the clinician. They love to talk about gambling - incessantly. They also use these discussions as a means of digression from more relevant discussions.
4. Be prepared for several missed appointments or last-minute cancellations. During the first session, establish a firm policy and clear statement about consequences for missed appointments.
5. Require at least a partial fee payment at each session. Pathological gamblers find it difficult not to turn fee payment into a game that favors them. This is a case in which it is truly therapeutic to require the client to make regular payment for services rendered.
6. Remain alert to the possibility of the client developing a cross-addiction as a replacement for gambling. Increased use of alcohol, food, or drugs is definitely a great risk for recovering gamblers.
7. Anticipate episodes of anxiety, depression, criticism of the value of therapy, and other such behavior around periods of significant sports events (e.g., World Series, championship boxing matches, Super Bowl Sunday, or Triple Crown

racing). This is especially common during the first year of abstinence.
8. Keep the first three to five sessions very structured and goal oriented. Use these sessions to confront the client in a constructive way with very concrete problems that have resulted from gambling. Be very task oriented about changes that must be made to overcome the problems.
9. Do not waste time trying to convince the problem gambler that in the long run the odds cannot be beaten. They know; they just do not care.
10. Keep the pathological gambler's significant family members involved in therapy, at least to some extent. If they were involved during inpatient care, continue their involvement. If they were not involved before, explain to the client the reasons to involve them and proceed to include them in ways you judge appropriate for the achievement of treatment goals.

One final cautionary comment should be made regarding the treatment of pathological gamblers. Only recently has the lack of control over gambling and its attendant adverse consequences been generally viewed as a psychological *disorder*. The inclusion of Pathological Gambling in the *DSM-III* and *DSM-III-R* as a distinct diagnostic category has legitimized psychological research aimed at identifying a causal basis for the disorder as well as the development of effective procedures for its treatment and cure. Current information on both etiology and proper treatment is tentative and incomplete. Although increasing numbers of clinicians have experience in treating pathological gamblers, there are as yet no true experts. It is important for clinicians who are treating pathological gamblers to appreciate the value of their own clinical observations and insights as a source of improved conceptualization and treatment of this disorder in the future.

REFERENCES

Abt, V., & McGurrin, M. C. (1984). Gambling: The misunderstood sport - A problem in social definition. *Leisure Sciences, 6*, 205-220.

Abt, V., & McGurrin, M. C. (1989). Toward a social science of addiction: A critical analysis of the disease model of addictive gambling. *Sociological Viewpoints, 5*, 75-86.

Abt, V., McGurrin, M. C., & Smith, J. F. (1985). Toward a synoptic model of gambling behavior. *Journal of Gambling Behavior, 1*, 79-88.

Abt, V., Smith, J. F., & Christiansen, E. M. (1985). *The Business of Risk: Commercial Gambling in Mainstream America*. Lawrence, KS: University of Kansas Press.

Abt, V., Smith, J. F., & McGurrin, M. C. (1985). Ritual, risk and reward: A role analysis of race track and casino encounters. *Journal of Gambling Behavior, 1*, 64-75.

Allcock, C., & Dickerson, M. (1986). *The Guide to Good Gambling*. Wentworth Falls, Australia: Social Science Press.

American Psychiatric Association. (1980). *Diagnostic and Statistical Manual of Mental Disorders* (3rd ed.). Washington, DC: Author.

American Psychiatric Association. (1987). *Diagnostic and Statistical Manual of Mental Disorders* (3rd ed. rev.). Washington, DC: Author.

Ashton, N. (1979). Gamblers - disturbed or healthy. In D. Lester (Ed.), *Gambling Today* (pp. 147-160). Springfield, IL: Charles C. Thomas.

Barker, J. C. (1968). Aversion therapy for compulsive gambling. *Journal of Nervous Mental Disease, 146*, 285-302.

Beattie, M. (1987). *Codependent No More.* New York: Harper & Row (Hazelden Series).

Bergler, E. (1957). *The Psychology of Gambling.* New York: Hill and Wang.

Blakey, G. R. (1979). State conducted lotteries: History, problems and promises. *Journal of Social Issues, 35*, 62-86.

Blume, S. B. (1988). Compulsive gambling and the medical model. *Journal of Gambling Behavior, 3*, 237-247.

Bolen, D. W., & Boyd, W. H. (1968). Gambling and the gamblers. *Archives of General Psychiatry, 18*, 617-630.

Branchey, L., Shaw, S., & Lieber, C. S. (1981). Ethanol impairs tryptophan transport into the brain and depresses serotonin. *Life Sciences, 29*, 2751-2755.

Brown, R. I. F. (1984, May). *Gamblers Anonymous' View of Its Own Success Rate as a Baseline for the Comparisons of Treatments of Compulsive Gamblers.* Paper presented at the Sixth National Conference on Gambling and Risk-Taking, Atlantic City, NJ.

Brown, R. I. F. (1986). Dropouts and continuers in Gamblers Anonymous: Life - context and other factors. *Journal of Gambling Behavior, 2*, 130-140.

Brown, R. I. F. (1988). Models of gambling and gambling addictions as perceptual filters. *Journal of Gambling Behavior, 3*, 224-236.

Burglass, M. E. (1989). Compulsive gambling: Forensic update and commentary. In H. J. Shaffer, S. A. Stein, B. Gambino, & T. N. Cummings (Eds.), *Compulsive Gambling: Theory, Research, and Practice* (pp. 205-222). Lexington, MA: D.C. Heath & Co.

Carlton, P. L., & Goldstein, L. (1987). Physiological determinants of pathological gambling. In T. Glaski (Ed.), *A Handbook of Pathological Gambling* (pp. 657-663). Springfield, IL: Charles C. Thomas.

Carlton, P. L., & Manowitz, P. (1988). Physiological factors as determinants of pathological gambling. *Journal of Gambling Behavior, 3*, 274-285.

Ciarrocchi, J. (1987). Severity of impairment in dually addicted gamblers. *Journal of Gambling Behavior, 3*, 16-26.

Commission on the Review of the National Policy Toward Gambling: Gambling in America. (1978). Washington, DC: U.S. Government Printing Office.

Compact Edition of the Oxford English Dictionary (1971). Oxford, England: University Press.

Corney, W. J., & Cummings, W. T. (1985). Gambling behavior and information processing biases. *Journal of Gambling Behavior, 1,* 64-75.

Cornish, D. B. (1978). *Gambling - A Review of the Literature and Its Implications for Policy and Research.* London, England: HMSO.

Culleton, R. P. (1985). *A Survey of Pathological Gamblers in the State of Ohio.* Columbus, OH: Report prepared for the Ohio Lottery Commission.

Culleton, R. P., & Lang, M. H. (1985). *The Prevalence Rate of Pathological Gambling in the Delaware Valley in 1984.* Camden, NJ: Forum for Policy Research and Public Service, Rutgers University.

Custer, R. L. (1986). An overview of compulsive gambling. In S.J. Levy & S. B. Blume (Eds.), *Addictions in the Jewish Community.* New York: Federation of Jewish Philanthropies.

Dickerson, M. G. (1984). *Compulsive Gamblers.* London, England: Longman.

Dickerson, M. G. (1988). The future of gambling research: Learning from the lessons of alcoholism. *Journal of Gambling Behavior, 3,* 248-256.

Dickerson, M. G., & Hinchy, J. (1987). The prevalence of excessive and pathological gambling in Australia. *Journal of Gambling Behavior, 3,* 191-211.

Dunne, J. A. (1985). Increasing public awareness of pathological gambling behavior: A history of the National Council on Compulsive Gambling. *Journal of Gambling Behavior, 1,* 8-15.

Fleming, A. M. (1978). *Something for Nothing: A History of Gambling.* New York: Delacorte Press.

Franklin, J., & Ciarrocchi, J. (1987). The team approach: Developing an experimental knowledge base for the treatment of the pathological gambler. *Journal of Gambling Behavior, 3,* 60-67.

Franklin, J., & Thoms, D. R. (1989). Clinical observation of family members of compulsive gamblers. In H. J. Shaffer, S.A. Stein, B. Gambino, & T. N. Cummings (Eds.), *Compulsive Gambling: Theory, Research, and Practice* (pp. 135-146). Lexington, MA: D.C. Heath & Co.

Gamblers Anonymous. (1980). *Twenty Questions.* Los Angeles, CA: Author.

Goldstein, L., Manowitz, P., Nora, R., Swartzburg, M., & Carlton, P. I. (1985). Differential EEG activation and pathological gambling. *Biological Psychiatry, 20*, 1232-1234.

Goodwin, F. K., & Post, R. M. (1983). 5-Hydroxytryptamine and depression: A model for the interaction of normal variance with pathology. *British Journal of Clinical Pharmacology, 15*, 3935-4055.

Goorney, A. B. (1968). Treatment of a compulsive horse race gambler by aversion therapy. *British Journal of Psychiatry, 114*, 329-333.

Greenberg, H. (1980). Psychology of gambling. In H. Kaplan, A. Freedman, & B. Sadock (Eds.), *Comprehensive Textbook of Psychiatry III* (pp. 3274-3283). New York: Williams and Wilkins.

Halliday, J., & Fuller, P. (1974). *The Psychology of Gambling*. London, England: Allen Lane.

Harvey, J. A., & Yunger, L. M. (1973). Relationship between telencephalic content and serotonin and pain sensitivity. In J. Barchas & E. Usdin (Eds.), *Serotonin and Behavior* (pp. 179-189). New York: Academic.

Huizinga, J. (1955). *Homo Ludens: A Study of the Play-Element in Culture*. Boston: Beacon.

Ingram, R. (1985). Transactional script theory applied to the pathological gambler. *Journal of Gambling Behavior, 1*, 89-91.

Jacobs, D. F. (1986). A general theory of addictions: A new theoretical model. *Journal of Gambling Behavior, 2*, 15-31.

Jacobs, D. F. (1988). Evidence for a common dissociative-like reaction among addicts. *Journal of Gambling Behavior, 4*, 27-37.

Jacobs, D. F. (1989). Teenage gambling. In H. J. Shaffer, S. A. Stein, B. Gambino, & T. N. Cummings (Eds.), *Compulsive Gambling,* (pp. 249-292). Lexington, MA: D.C. Heath & Co.

Jacobs, D. F., & Kuley, N. B. (1987). *High School Gambling*. Unpublished research report, Jerry L. Pettis Memorial Veterans Hospital, Loma Linda, CA.

Kallick, M., Suits, D., Dielman, T., & Hybels, J. (1979). *A Survey of American Gambling Attitudes and Behavior*. Ann Arbor, MI: Survey Research Center, Institute for Social Research.

Kuley, N. B., & Jacobs, D. F. (1988). The relationship between dissociative-like experiences and sensation seeking among social and problem gamblers. *Journal of Gambling Behavior, 3*, 190-198.

Kusyszyn, I. (1978). Compulsive gambling: The problem of definition. *International Journal of Addictions, 13,* 1095-1101.

Kusyszyn, I., & Rubenstein, L. (1985). Locus of control and race track betting behaviors: A preliminary investigation. *Journal of Gambling Behavior, 1,* 106-110.

Lesieur, H. (1979). Compulsive gambler's spiral of options and involvement. *Psychiatry, 42,* 79-87.

Lesieur, H. R., & Blume, S. (1987). The South Oaks Gambling Screen (SOGS): A new instrument for the identification of pathological gamblers. *American Journal of Psychiatry, 144,* 1184-1188.

Lesieur, H. R., & Custer, R. L. (1984). Pathological gambling: Roots, phases, and treatment. *Annals of American Academy of Political and Social Sciences, 474,* 146-156.

Lesieur, H. R., & Klein, R. (1987). Pathological gambling among high school students. *Addictive Behaviors, 12,* 129-135.

Lester, D. (1980). The treatment of compulsive gambling. *International Journal of the Addictions, 15,* 201-206.

Lieberman, L. (1988). *A Social Typology of Gambling Behavior: Suggestions for a Short Screening Device.* New York: National Council of Compulsive Gambling.

Martinez, T. (1975). A review of gambling: Hazard and reward. *Society, 12,* 88-89.

Martinez, T. (1983). *The Gambling Scene.* Springfield, IL: Charles C. Thomas.

McCormick, R. A., Russo, A. M., Ramirez, L. F., & Taber, J. I. (1984). Affective disorders among pathological gamblers seeking treatment. *American Journal of British Psychiatry, 141,* 215-218.

McGurrin, M. C. (1986, March). *Personality Characteristics of Pathological Gamblers.* Paper presented at the First National Conference on Gambling Behavior, New York.

McGurrin, M. C. (1989). *Treatment Applications in Controlled Gambling Models of Pathological Gambling.* Paper presented at the Fourth National Conference on Gambling Behavior, Des Moines, IA.

McGurrin, M. C., Abt, V., & Smith, J. F. (1984). Play or pathology: A new look at the gambler and his world. In B. Smoth (Ed.), *The Masks of Play* (pp. 24-36). West Point, NY: Leisure Press.

Miller, W. (1986). Individual outpatient treatment of pathological gambling. *Journal of Gambling Behavior, 2,* 95-107.

Moody, G. (1972). The facts about the money factories. *London Churches Council on Gambling, 1*, 95-107.

Nadler, L. B. (1985). The epidemiology of pathological gambling: Critique of existing research and alternative strategies. *Journal of Gambling Behavior, 1*, 35-50.

Naranjo, C. A., Sellers, E. M., & Lawrin, M. O. (1986). Modulation of ethanol intake by serotonin uptake inhibitors. *Journal of Clinical Psychiatry, 47*, 16-22.

National Council on Problem Gambling. (1989). 445 West 59th Street, New York, NY 10019. Telephone: (212) 765-3833.

Nemzer, E. D., Arnold, L. E., Votolato, N. A., & McConnell, H. (1986). Amino acid supplementation as therapy for attention deficit disorder. *Journal of the American Academy of Child Psychiatry, 25*, 509-513.

Oldman, D. (1974). Chance and skill: A study of roulette. *Sociology, 8*, 407-426.

Oldman, D. (1978). Compulsive gamblers. *Sociological Review, 26*, 349-370.

Orford, J. (1985). *Excessive Appetites: A Psychological View of Addictions*. New York: Wiley.

Peele, S. (1984). The cultural context of psychological approaches to alcoholism. *American Psychologist, 39*, 1337-1351.

Preston, F. W., & Smith, R. W. (1985). Delabeling and relabeling in Gamblers Anonymous: Problems with transferring the Alcoholics Anonymous paradigm. *Journal of Gambling Behavior, 1*, 97-105.

Ramirez, L. F., McCormick, R. A., Russo, A. M., & Taber, J. I. (1984). Patterns of substance abuse in pathological gamblers undergoing treatment. *Addictive Behaviors, 8*, 425-428.

Rankin, H. (1982). Control rather than abstinence as a goal in the treatment of excessive gambling. *Behavior Research Therapy, 20*, 185-187.

Rosecrance, J. (1985). Compulsive gambling and the medicalization of deviance. *Social Problems, 32*, 275-284.

Rosecrance, J. (1989). Controlled gambling: A promising future. In H. J. Shaffer, S. A. Stein, B. Gambino, & T. N. Cummings (Eds.), *Compulsive Gambling* (pp. 147-160). Lexington, MA: D.C. Heath & Co.

Rosenthal, R. J. (1986). The pathological gambler's system for self-deception. *Journal of Gambling Behavior, 2*, 108-120.

Rotter, J. B. (1966). Generalized expectancies for internal versus external control of reinforcement. *Psychological Monographs, 80,* 1(Whole No. 609).

Scodel, A. (1964). Inspirational group therapy: A study of Gamblers Anonymous. *American Journal of Psychotherapy, 18,* 1115-1125.

Seagar, C. (1970). Treatment of compulsive gamblers by electric aversion. *British Journal of Psychiatry, 117,* 545-553.

Shaffer, H. S., Stein, S., Gambino, B., & Cummings, T. N. (1989). *Compulsive Gambling: Theory, Research, and Practice.* Lexington, MA: D.C. Heath & Co.

Smith v. United States, 36 F.2d. 548 (D.C. Cir. 1929).

Steinberg, M. (1988, May). *Gambling Behavior Among High School Students in Connecticut.* Paper presented at the Third National Conference on Gambling, National Council on Compulsive Gambling, New York.

Strachan, M. L. (1989). Women gamblers - the difference. *Quarterly News from the National Council on Compulsive Gambling, 4,* 10-11.

Taber, J. I. (1988). Compulsive gambling: An examination of relevant models. *Journal of Gambling Behavior, 3,* 219-223.

Taber, J. I., Russo, A. M., Adkins, B. J., & McCormick, R. A. (1986). Ego strength and achievement motivation in pathological gamblers. *Journal of Gambling Behavior, 2,* 69-80.

Tepperman, J. H. (1985). The effectiveness of short-term group therapy upon the pathological gambler and wife. *Journal of Gambling Behavior, 1,* 119-130.

United States v. Gould, 741 F.2d. 45, 52 (4th Cir. 1984).

United States v. Lewellyn, 723 F.2d. 615, 619 (8th Cir. 1983).

United States v. Pomponio, 429 U.S. 10 (1976).

United States v. Shorter, 608 F. Supp. 871 (D.D.C. 1985).

United States v. Shorter, 618 F. Supp. 255 (D.D.C. 1987).

United States v. Torniero, 735 F.2d. 725, 730 (2nd Cir. 1984).

Volberg, R. (1989). Report on a five-state study. *Quarterly News from the National Council on Compulsive Gambling, 4,* 7-8.

Volberg, R. A., & Steadman, H. J. (1988). Refining prevalence estimates of pathological gambling. *American Journal of Psychiatry, 145,* 502-505.

Volberg, R. A., & Steadman, H. J. (1989). Policy implications of prevalence estimates of pathological gambling. In H. J. Shaffer, S. A. Stein, B. Gambino, & T. N. Cummings (Eds.),

Compulsive Gambling (pp. 163-174). Lexington, MA: D.C. Heath & Co.

Weissman, A. (1973). Behavioral pharmacology of p-chlorophenylaline (PCPA). In J. Barchas & E. Usdin (Eds.), *Serotonin and Behavior* (pp. 235-248). New York: Academic.

Wender, P. H., Reimherr, F. W., & Wood, D. R. (1981). Attention deficit disorder (minimal brain dysfunction) in adults. *Archives of General Psychiatry, 38*, 449-456.

Wexler, S. (1984, May). *A Chart on the Effects of Compulsive Gambling on the Wife.* Paper presented at the Sixth National Conference on Gambling and Risk-Taking, Atlantic City, NJ.

Wood, D. R., Wender, P. H., & Reimherr, F. W. (1983). The prevalence of attention deficit disorder, residual type, or minimal brain dysfunction in a population of male alcoholic patients. *American Journal of Psychiatry, 140*, 95-98.

Young, S. N. (1986). The clinical psychopharmacology of tryptophan. In R. J. Wurtman & J. J. Wurtman (Eds.), *Nutrition and the Brain* (pp. 49-88). New York: Raven.

Young, S. N., Smith, S. E., Pihl, R. O., & Ervin, F. R. (1985). Tryptophan depletion causes a rapid lowering of mood in normal males. *Psychopharmacology, 87*, 173-177.

NOTES

NOTES

Some Of The Other Titles Available From Professional Resource Press

Innovations in Clinical Practice: A Source Book - **10 Volumes**
    Hardbound edition (Vols. 3-10 only) per volume.. $54.20
    Looseleaf binder edition (Vols. 1-10) per volume... $59.20
Cognitive Therapy with Couples... $17.70
Maximizing Third-Party Reimbursement in Your Mental Health Practice................. $32.70
Who Speaks for the Children?
    The Handbook of Individual and Class Child Advocacy....................................... $43.70
Post-Traumatic Stress Disorder:
    Assessment, Differential Diagnosis, and Forensic Evaluation............................ $27.70
Clinical Evaluations of School-Aged Children: A Structured Approach to
    the Diagnosis of Child and Adolescent Mental Disorders.................................... $22.70
Stress Management Training: A Group Leader's Guide.. $14.70
Stress Management Workbook for Law Enforcement Officers...................................... $ 8.70
Fifty Ways to Avoid Malpractice:
    A Guidebook for Mental Health Professionals... $17.70
Keeping Up the Good Work:
    A Practitioner's Guide to Mental Health Ethics.. $16.70
Think Straight! Feel Great! 21 Guides to Emotional Self-Control................................ $14.70
Computer-Assisted Psychological Evaluations:
    How to Create Testing Programs in BASIC... $22.70

Titles In Our Practitioner's Resource Series

Assessment and Treatment of Multiple Personality and Dissociative Disorders • Clinical Guidelines for Involuntary Outpatient Treatment • Cognitive Therapy for Personality Disorders: A Schema-Focused Approach • Dealing with Anger Problems: Rational-Emotive Therapeutic Interventions • Diagnosis and Treatment Selection for Anxiety Disorders • Neuropsychological Evaluation of Head Injury • Outpatient Treatment of Child Molesters • Pathological Gambling: Conceptual, Diagnostic, and Treatment Issues •Pre-Employment Screening for Psychopathology: A Guide to Professional Practice• *Tarasoff* and Beyond: Legal and Clinical Considerations in the Treatment of Life-Endangering Patients • What Every Therapist Should Know about AIDS

All books in this series are $11.70 each

All prices include shipping charges. Foreign orders add $2.00 shipping to total. All orders from individuals and private institutions must be prepaid in full. Florida residents add 7% sales tax. Prices and availability subject to change without notice.

See Reverse Side For Ordering Information ⟶

To Order

To order by mail, please send name, address, and telephone number, along with check or credit card information (card number and expiration date) to:

**Professional Resource Press
PO Box 15560
Sarasota, FL 34277-1560**

For fastest service
(VISA/MasterCard/American Express/Discover orders only)
CALL 1-813-366-7913 or FAX 1-813-366-7971

Would You Like To Be On Our Mailing List?

If so, please write, call, or fax the following information:

Name:_____

Address:_____

Address:_____

City/State/Zip:_____

To insure that we send you all appropriate mailings, please include your professional affiliation (e.g., psychologist, clinical social worker, marriage and family therapist, mental health counselor, school psychologist, psychiatrist, nurse, etc.).